Every Highway

RIDING SHOTGUN IN THE BIG RIGS

Library and Archives Canada Cataloguing in Publication

Feschuk, Dave
    Every highway : riding shotgun in the big rigs / Dave Feschuk.

ISBN 13: 978-0-7710-4750-3
ISBN 10: 0-7710-4750-9

1. Truck drivers – North America.   2. Trucking – North America.
I. Title.

HD8039.M7952N67 2006   388.3'24'097   C2005-907315-2

We acknowledge the financial support of the Government of Canada through the Book Publishing Industry Development Program and that of the Government of Ontario through the Ontario Media Development Corporation's Ontario Book Initiative. We further acknowledge the support of the Canada Council for the Arts and the Ontario Arts Council for our publishing program.

Some people's names in this book have been changed to respect their privacy.

Excerpt on page 16 from *The Grapes of Wrath* by John Steinbeck, copyright 1939, renewed © 1967 by John Steinbeck. Used by permission of Viking Penguin, a division of Penguin Group (USA) Inc.

Every effort has been made to reach the copyright holders of material excerpted in this book.

Typeset in Minion by M&S, Toronto
Printed and bound in Canada

This book is printed on acid-free paper that is 100% recycled, ancient-forest friendly (100% post-consumer recycled).

McClelland & Stewart Ltd.
75 Sherbourne Street
Toronto, Ontario
M5A 2P9
www.mcclelland.com

1   2   3   4   5   10   09   08   07   06

For Andrea

Contents

Introduction

My cousin Lo quit his job as a truck driver a couple of years back. He was sick of the long hours and the paltry pay, and of sleep so infrequent that he had to strategically set a series of alarm clocks to ensure he was suitably roused. Chief among the alarms, which he placed in different corners of his truck so he would have to rise from the tiny bunk behind his driver's seat to turn them off, was the Screamin' Meanie. Its screech measures 100 decibels – it's akin to waking up with your head snuggled close to the engine end of a working lawn mower. It's the safest wake-up assurance thirty dollars can buy. The first alarm goes for five minutes. The second one goes for ten minutes. Both alarms can be silenced with the push of a snooze button. But the third and final alarm doesn't stop blaring unless three separate buttons are pushed simultaneously. Lo claimed the Meanie, which comes in a package with the tag line, "Do Not Use Near Graveyards. May Wake

Dead!" was the only device he could count on to interrupt his slumbers.

In his truck-stop dreams he would often see flashes passing before his eyes. "A white line, a white line, a white line, a white line . . ." When he wanted to emphasize for me how exhausted he had become – how his entire life was based on delivering his cargo while denying his chronic grogginess – he'd deadpan those words until I nodded sympathetically. But I wasn't the one who'd cheated sleep by belting Hank Williams with my head out the window in a North Dakota blizzard. I'd never popped uppers to make it through upstate New York; never quaffed six coffees and pissed into a can as I cranked it for the Quebec border. I couldn't really understand.

Lo, who had done all those things – or told stories as though he had – hauled freight across the continent for more than five years, during which time his only consistent companions were a cassette deck and a six-string guitar with which he alternately listened to and composed a canon of country-music songs. Whenever I'd see him – every handful of months, when he made a one- or two-night stop in our hometown, and only then when he wasn't too tired to venture out to a local pub or a family get-together – I marvelled at his vast knowledge of twangy standards, and at the honest beauty of his own tunes. He sang of breakdowns on desolate roads; of breakups with girlfriends back home; of the heavy loads that weighed on his fifty-three-foot trailer and his thirty-one-year-old mind. And before he launched into his best numbers during his rare gigs, he'd attach this invariable segue, lest anyone doubt the authenticity of his muse: "... It got me thinking," he'd say, summing up some tale from his travels to the forty-eight contiguous states and ten Canadian provinces, "so I hopped into the back of my truck and I wrote this song."

For him it began as a summer job, paying the university bills by doing local deliveries for an agricultural company based in Beamsville, Ontario. Local, in this instance, meant the entire province of Ontario. It meant driving a pickup truck to Tillsonburg and Windsor, Ottawa and Napanee. He wasn't yet a trucker, but life on the move was making an impression. "It reminded me of everything that I had ever loved about road trips with my father when I was young," he once wrote to me. "The age-old saying, 'The destination is only surpassed by the journey,' all of a sudden meant something." In those long university summers, which stretched from May through August, he hung around with truck drivers after work. He learned their trade over truck-stop coffee and tavern draft. And he learned to drive a tractor-trailer in a seat he still remembers, that of a new 1994 Mack CH Custom Elite double sleeper with all the trimmings.

"I can still feel that shifter. I can still smell that truck," he says. "I was doing this to pay for my education. Little did I know it would enhance it."

He finished school (a geography degree with an eye, he told people, toward teaching). But life took a turn. It was about a girl, a girl everybody I knew thought he'd marry. At the end, after the breakup, he hit the road.

His first long-haul voyage took him east through Ontario, Quebec, New Brunswick, and Nova Scotia, a run he'd come to make often. He still remembers watching the sunset from the Cartier Bridge in Montreal, the sun rise over the Saint John and the Saint Lawrence rivers. He talks of picking apples off the roadside trees in the Annapolis Valley, of running illegally through the top of New Brunswick (on Highway 108) by driving longer in a day than the law allows just so he could see the Miramichi River in its entirety. He saw so many sights, and he saw them alone.

"I was laid over in Phoenix, an hour out of Flagstaff, Arizona. I was there two days and I was like, 'I'm going to go up to the Grand Canyon.' But then I was like, 'Fuck that. I've seen all this beautiful country on my own.' I wanted to go up to the Grand Canyon so bad, but I stayed in my truck . . . I just didn't want to see another beautiful thing by myself."

It wasn't long after that that he quit the road. But like a lot of truckers, he and the tarmac, the man and his beloved machine, carry on a complicated relationship. After a short return to the driver's seat – after a few more months of twenty-hour days and Screamin' Meanie sunrises – he was sitting at the dispatcher's desk, and he remained there, coordinating the pickup and drop-off of shipments, for a while before changing careers. But the urge to roam never seems to leave him. People ask him to this day if he misses being in the truck. "I tell 'em, 'Only every other day,'" he says, laughing. "Don't ever be surprised if you get a call from me and I say, 'I'm back on the road.' Because I imagine one day I'll find myself there."

For my part, I've been waiting anxiously for that day. Always game for a road trip, it's one of my great regrets that I never rode shotgun in Lo's big Mack. He offered the seat more than once, and though the timing never worked, my curiosity about the truck-driving life never abated. And so I am setting out to satisfy my hankering, riding alongside a handful of truck drivers on roads from the Subarctic to Southern California. Along the way I'll attempt to get a look inside their lives and inside their rigs, and to these pages I'll commit my notes from the road.

I am no trucker. I am a sportswriter. But the occupations have their similarities. I occasionally spend consecutive days, sometimes weeks, away from home in service to my employer. I have deadlines that don't meet with my definition of reasonable. I eat beige meals under fluorescent lights alongside disgruntled colleagues whose complaints about the business, some certified beef, some crotchety folly, are constant and peppered with humour and genuine hurt. Just like a truck stop, the press room has foul mouths and large bellies in quantity; failing marriages and failing bodies; successful entrepreneurs and pseudo business types; hangovers heaped with coffee and storytellers fuelled by the alco-caffeine buzz.

But, as my cousin says, "Driving truck's like nothing else." And I don't claim to know the fine points of the pavement. The most truck-like vehicle I have ever driven is the rusty 1983 Volvo sedan I recently left for dead at a garage after a frustrating three-day span in a particularly harsh December during which the brakes failed, the radiator burst, and, worst of all in teeth-chattering throes of a northland winter, the heater blew cold. I had purchased said Volvo three years earlier for $1,000 on the recommendation of a friend who swore by the Swedish-built boxes because they were easy to fix, and because he had once been driving one – a baby blue coupe circa 1978 – on the day he survived a head-on crash with a truck on a two-lane highway. Just as my friend began the search for another Volvo the next day, I replaced my beloved '83 with a '92.

Since travelling, and not necessarily driving, is a passion, I will be more than happy to occupy the passenger seat, seeing the world through the high-riding windshield of a four-hundred-horsepower mammoth. I have chosen to travel with truckers, to mine their stories and probe their feelings, because their work is more important than most people know. Although the railroad built North America, joining it from coast to coast, the roads renovate it, feed it, clothe it, and employ it. Trucks dominate the transportation business in Canada, moving about 90 per cent of all domestic consumer products and foodstuffs, shipping out about 60 per cent of our exports to the States, bringing in more than 80 per cent of the imports. Truck driver was the most common occupation of Canadian men according to Canada's 2001 census. Somewhere – everywhere, it seems – there is a truck rumbling down a highway, and another truck riding its bumper, and probably another riding yours. But while trucks are as ubiquitous as the potholes they chew – and while their drivers are often resented for clogging our automotive arteries – most people don't know much about the goings-on inside those massive cabs.

Truck drivers have had better moments in history. They were once romanticized as heroes of the endless black ribbon. Humphrey Bogart, the actor who would be named the greatest male film star of all time by the American Film Institute in 1999, once played a Depression-era trucker admirably fighting the system in *They Drive by Night*. In *The Grapes of Wrath*, John Steinbeck's 1939 novel, truckers are the centre of the author's vivid portrait of hamburger-stand culture along Route 66, the migratory trail that takes waves of Americans to the burgeoning promised land of the West. In Steinbeck's diner, truck drivers are feted by the staff as "the backbone of the joint. Where the trucks stop, that's where the customers come. Can't fool truck drivers, they know. They bring the customers. They know. Give 'em a stale cup of coffee an' they're off the joint. Treat 'em right an' they come back." While the dispossessed migrants of the dust-bowl Midwest are cast as undesirables and thieves, truckers drink their java and eat pineapple cream pie and bring prosperity.

The lives of truckers have taken a drastic turn. Free trade and government deregulation have made it a different game since the so-called trucking craze of the late 1970s and early 1980s, when movies such as *Smokey and the*

Bandit and *Convoy* played on North America's big screens
and trucking slang – "ten-four," "breaker-breaker" –
infiltrated the popular tongue. Back then, the trucker still
had an honourable public image. He was known as the
benevolent man of the highway, a knight of the road,
revered by the stranded motorists he rescued; admired by
road-tripping children with noses pressed to the back-seat
glass, for whom he offered a friendly blast of his air horn.
Truckers were even invited for dinner by rural residents
on regular routes. These days, there are more than ten times
as many truckers and no such respect.

Even before I set out, I know that change abounds
behind the wheel. The CB (citizens' band radio) remains a
cheap and practical communication tool, but drivers stay
in touch with the world via e-mail and cellphones and satellite-linked computers and global-positioning systems, and
so even on the emptiest stretches of tundra, they're never
really alone. Computers in, say, a Toronto suburb can
monitor a truck's vital statistics – its speed, its fuel con-
sumption – no matter how far it roams. The technology
exists so that a supervisor in the same industrial-park office
can shut down an engine that is thousands of miles away
with a click of a mouse, all without the driver's permission.

A 2002 advertisement for the U.S. fuel company
Chevron summed up the plight of the overworked trucker,
on whom the pressure to deliver never abates. The ad,
which appeared in the trucking trade magazines, featured a
photo of a handsome young man standing in front of a

gleaming rig with the caption: "Welcome to the twelve-day week, rookie." Two- and three-day journeys come with arrival times estimated to the minute, and some drivers have complained that they feel as supervised as a worker on a factory floor; that the days of far-flung freedom are over. But it largely remains a loner's life. There's still plenty of downtime in unfamiliar ports; still many hours to write songs or find companionship or pine for home.

And there is still enough societal demonization of the trucking business for many truckers to feel self-conscious about their jobs. In *Duel* (1971), the first movie directed by Steven Spielberg, a motorist played by Dennis Weaver finds himself in a quandary. He is late for an appointment, driving on a California freeway. And to make matters worse, he is stuck behind a slow-moving tanker truck that is belching fumes into his open window. Weaver's short-sleeved character, David Mann, hits the gas of his red Plymouth Valiant and passes the truck, a dirty, rusty Peterbilt 351 tanker with a windshield so soiled that the driver is unidentifiable. For a moment, Mann is free to go on his speedy way. But suddenly the once-plodding tanker finds a burst of speed. It passes Mann, only to resume its slow pace. And as the camera catches the word emblazoned on the truck's rear end – FLAMMABLE – Mann gets hot. He floors the accelerator, passes the truck yet again, and doesn't slow down until he stops at a gas station up the road. The cat-and-mouse game ensues for the rest of the film. The anonymous psycho trucker – seemingly the embodiment of not only Mann's, but Everyman's, worst fears – is eventually responsible for untold mayhem. The unsuspecting motorist is an inexplicable victim of the evil that surely lurks within every denizen of the big rigs.

Truckers have been portrayed as menacing nuisances, if not psychotic killers, many times since. Luxury car commercials feature sleek machines emerging from the foreboding shadows of smoke-spewing semis. An ad for a Mercedes-Benz sport-utility vehicle bragged that even "mean old truckers" couldn't dissuade the mighty M-Class from its rightful place on the road. The entire phenomenon of the SUV and the luxury pickup truck can arguably be traced to the desire of drivers to sit higher above the road, all to feel more secure in the presence of the motorized mammoths. That ad was promptly taken off the air at least in part because of the lobbying efforts of Loved Ones and Drivers Support (LOADS), a watchdog group that, in the late 1990s, took up the cause of calling out companies that used negative stereotypes of truckers to move product. Despite their status as an irreplaceable cog in the economy, many truckers continue to complain of being decried as a lamentable scourge. And perhaps that's because a 1991 Royal Commission into transportation found that each tractor-trailer in Canada costs the taxpayer about ten thousand dollars in road-maintenance bills per annum that aren't recouped in taxes and licensing fees. Perhaps it's because the culture remains gritty at some truck stops and rest areas, where nearby strip bars and prostitution rings are especially profitable roadside enterprises. But even the off-ramp oasis is being gentrified. The super-stops near the busiest border checkpoints – where a truck crosses the Canada–U.S. boundary every 2.5 seconds – are spectacles of corporate wholesomeness catering to the users of recreational vehicles and automobiles as much as to truckers. Some of them come with bowling alleys and yuppie-approved latte shops, health-food stores, fitness clubs, and marble-tiled shower stalls, the trademark of one popular truck-stop purveyor, modelled after the luxurious bathing facilities in Ritz-Carlton hotels. There are those who lament the slow elimination of their trade's former staples, the things that made the job worth doing. The out-of-the-way diners and their pot-holed gravel parking lots are giving way to the slick monoliths who cater as much to devotees of recreational vehicles as they do to the professional drivers who built their empires. The smiling diner waitresses are taking jobs at the mega-stops, or at Wal-Mart, another popular stop for the modern trucker seeking ample parking near the highway and low prices and a universe of selection. But the industry keeps piling forward, the profit margins ever slimmer, the competition evermore fierce.

"The days of the trucking cowboy are gone," a trucking lobbyist once told me. "A lot of the old-time images of the noble loner are gone. These guys don't have time to be saving stranded motorists like in the movies. They've got to be businessmen."

Many, of course, aren't businessmen. But the truckers, en masse, keep delivering. Their pay often gets lower as

fuel prices rise, their travels lose their romance as the dead-
line-pressure looms. They are fined by the authorities and
vilified in the media for working longer than they are
legally allowed to work, for driving tired. But their lifestyle
remains alluring enough to blanket the roads in big rigs,
to inspire me to begin this journey.

1

Born Again

The knights of the road walk with wobbles and limps, pigeon toes and bowed legs, descending from their mechanical steeds to hitch their pants, complain of arthritis on the knees or throbs in the lumbar. They wear triple-XL T-shirts like tents. They drink from quadruple-XL coffee mugs. And though Doan's pills, a drug once frequently employed to quell pain and inflammation, aren't particularly popular these days, two decades after singer Dave Dudley wrote his lament of trucking's physical toll, "Rolaids, Doan's Pills and Preparation H," the gamut remains the standard of the truck-stop shelf. Indigestion and hemorrhoids remain occupational hazards, as do the creaky joints that seem to affect so many truckers of experience.

You can take notes on long-hauling gaits at truck stops around North America. I am taking mine on a hazy summer afternoon, the humid smog hanging southern Ontario in its usual choke hold, when a man bearing a striking resemblance to Popeye, the Sailor Man, taps the hood of my station wagon as he walks through the parking lot. He interrupts my writing down details of a conversation with a cattle-hauling trucker from Calgary whose cargo can still be heard mooing in the parking lot's dusty corner. My door is ajar, the windows are down. "Your lights are on," says the man, who has a cartoonish face, red-spot cheeks, formidable forearms, and even a sailor's cap, albeit the navy-blue Greek variety.

I say thanks, click them off, and watch him walk into a truck stop across a field from a nuclear power plant. Popeye walks with no ease, a side-to-side stutter that passes for a stride. But he makes it to the door and soon returns, squinting at the sun, sweating through his shirt.

And so we talk a while, he introducing himself as Korny, then as Denne Kornechuk of St. Marys, Ontario. I tell him I'm a -chuk, too.

"Ah, I can spot a Uke-a-rainian a mile away," he says.

Korny was born on Black Monday 1929, the same day stockbrokers evacuated Wall Street windows after a stock market crashed and the world's economy began its plummet into depression. Perhaps because of that, he has never owned a stock or a bond or a mutual fund. His investment was in property, a tree-shaded lot in the fruitlands west of Lake Ontario where he built a home with his wife, June. The property is paid for and remains his home. But June died fifteen years ago; Korny says it took him a few years to get over her passing, to stop carousing, to become, as he has, a born-again Christian who's as much an evangelist for trucking-industry change as he is for the Lord.

"Yep, yep," he says. "Trucking has gone all to rat shit. All to rat shit."

Here is the old hand's beef: He works ten hours a day, gets thirty-six cents a mile. He makes, by his own estimation – when he figures in the waiting in traffic and the waiting at the loading dock – about ten or eleven dollars an hour hauling truckloads for the Canadian arm of a U.S. trucking conglomerate. But here is the kicker: back in 1955, when he drove a tanker for Sunoco, delivering oil on a regular route that allowed him to sleep in his own bed every night and thereby witness the growth of his son, Thom, he made $12.50 an hour. The latter figure is not adjusted for inflation. It's a flat-out comparison: $12.50 in 1955 dollars would be worth about ninety dollars today. So a half-century has passed and Korny is making 13 per cent of what he once did. And if it weren't for his pension and his paid-off mortgage, he'd have quit long ago. As it is, he doesn't mind lamenting a bygone era.

"Back then trucking was a good-paying job, plus you were a somebody in the company at that time. Today you're just a number. Any one of these big transport companies, you're just a number," he says, wagging a finger. "You're a nothing in the company, whereas when I was with Sunoco in 1955 up to '79, I was a somebody. I had a bow tie. They supplied me with my clothes. I got holidays of all kinds. When they had banquets every year, you were a somebody.

Today you're dick all. That's the whole thing about trucking today. It's just a job.

"Our drivers, they're starving. They can't make it. They're driving them into the ground. Just recently we had one driver that fell asleep (to no harm). The fatigue gets you. Your eyes are wide open but you're looking in the mirror saying, 'Did I hit anyone?'"

In *The Grapes of Wrath*, Steinbeck tells the tale of a farming family's migration from its Oklahoma homestead to the promised land of California, observing as they do the rush of traffic to the continent's western edge.

"And along the highway there came a long line of huge freight trucks with red sides," writes Steinbeck. "They rumbled along, putting a little earthquake in the ground, and the standing exhaust pipes sputtered blue smoke from the Diesel oil. One man drove each truck, and his relief man slept in a bunk high up against the ceiling. But the trucks never stopped; they thundered day and night and the ground shook under their heavy march."

The ground hasn't stopped shaking along North America's highways. And Steinbeck's phrase – "the trucks never stopped" – isn't far from the truth. Until June of 2003, U.S. truckers were regulated by hours-of-service rules written in 1939, which allowed drivers ten hours behind the wheel at a time. The new rules, which were amended after calls for more attention to big-truck safety, allowed for fourteen consecutive on-duty hours with a maximum of eleven driving hours therein. They allowed for an on-duty schedule of sixty hours in seven days or seventy hours in eight days. They increased the required amount of off-duty time from eight hours to ten hours. There was also a so-called sleeper-berth exception that allowed drivers to accumulate the equivalent of ten consecutive off-duty hours by taking two separate rests in a sleeper berth, provided that neither rest period lasts less than two hours and that, when you combine the driving time in the period before and after each rest period, it doesn't amount to more than fourteen hours.

Canadian drivers can drive thirteen hours consecutively followed by an off-duty period of at least eight consecutive hours. They can't be on duty for more than sixty hours in a seven-day week, more than seventy hours in an eight-day period, or more than 120 hours in a fourteen-day string. They also can't accumulate more than seventy-five on-duty hours without a minimum of twenty-four hours off-duty.

The hours are long and, many sleep experts will tell you, they're unsustainable. The problem with sleep is that you can't really avoid it. There is but one solution to fatigue: sleep. Singing at the top of one's lungs with the windows open and the radio blasting does not invigorate the exhausted traveller. Sleep scientists say that tired drivers tend to have slower reaction time, less eye movement that translates to less awareness of their environment. They tend to weave in and out of lanes at higher rates than perfectly alert counterparts. There are circadian rhythms that have their way. The time of day has been found to be a better predictor of driver fatigue than the cumulative time behind the wheel. One study found that the incidence of drowsiness was eight times more frequent in the hours between midnight and 6 a.m.

In one survey taken at inspection stations 19 per cent of truckers reported falling asleep at least once, and in some cases more, in the past month. According to a 1997 study at the State University of New York, nearly half of the 3 million long-haul truckers in the United States and the two hundred thousand truckers in Canada have fallen asleep at the wheel at some point in their careers, and 25 per cent of truckers said they'd dozed off at least once in the previous year. In a study by the American Automobile Association, which examined 231 big-truck accidents that were serious enough that the truck had to be towed from the scene, it was estimated fatigue was the primary cause of 40 per cent of the accidents and had contributed to 60 per cent. When new hours-of-service rules were proposed in 2003, wherein Canadian drivers would have been permitted to drive six consecutive fourteen-hour shifts followed by a thirty-six-hour rest period that would allow them to restart another eighty-four-hour week, critics pointed out that the rules paid no heed to the differences between driving at night and driving during the day.

Some truckers have a difficult time sleeping on demand; studies have shown truckers typically average five hours of sleep a night, which experts say isn't nearly enough to avoid chronic fatigue. If they don't fall asleep behind the wheel, they sometimes fall into microsleep, involuntarily shutting their eyes for up to ten seconds at a time. Even a five-second shutdown of the eyelids means a truck travelling at sixty

miles per hour goes more than the length of a football field
without the benefit of human cognition.

Albert Labelle, for one, is a Winnipeg trucker whose out-
of-control rig killed an Alberta man who was driving his
pregnant wife and three-year-old daughter on a trip to the
zoo. In 2000, he stood outside an Edmonton courthouse and
effectively gave up his brethren in the trucking business.
Labelle had just pled guilty to three counts of driving more
than the legal limit and to falsifying his logbooks – charges
that weren't directly related to the fatal crash, for which pros-
ecutors could produce no evidence of Labelle's logbook
delinquency – when he stated his belief that it's impossible
for truckers to make a living by living within the law.

"You have no choice – it's do it or get another job,"
he said.

Korny isn't in the market for another job – not that his
is ideal. "As a man that's been behind the wheel for fifty-
one years, I say these trucking companies need to be fair
with the people. They're not. They're not fair to the people.
They're not fair to the drivers. And how do you expect
these accidents happen? Because these people are getting
fatigued and they want to make money – they're starving
out here – and they can't seem to get home, and they're on
the road for maybe a week or two weeks. It's ridiculous. I
just don't know how this could be justified.

"The only way is, they've got to pay more. Otherwise,
the driver is getting the finger stuck at him."

Indeed, Korny isn't alone in his opinion. Driver wages,
adjusted for inflation, haven't improved much since the

1950s. And ever since the U.S. industry was deregulated in 1980 – a move that made it far easier to start up a trucking business and precipitated the founding of thousands of small firms seeking to benefit from the new ease of entry and the freedom to set rates – it can be argued that the big winners have been the dominant handful of companies, which became all the more dominant.

Canadian deregulation – "economic regulatory reform" in the words of Ottawa's bureaucrats – happened on January 1, 1988, and brought with it a swell in new start-up companies. By 1991, the number of trucking firms had increased 600 per cent from 500 to 3,000. A $2-billion pie was evermore thinly sliced. For shippers, it was a godsend. For consumers, ditto. The price of moving goods kept dropping; the price of goods stayed low.

But some of the business-strapped companies started bidding at work below cost to maintain cashflow. And it didn't help that American companies were said to have an 18 per cent cost advantage over their Canadian competitors thanks to more favourable tax arrangements in their home states. So in the first eleven months of 1990, 130 Ontario trucking companies declared bankruptcy, a 132 per cent increase over the same period in 1989. In the United States, meanwhile, of the top fifty U.S. trucking companies that were operating in 1978, only nine were in existence by 1993. The rest had closed or merged.

"The only ones who benefited," says Korny, "were the biggest of the big. Us little guys, we got nothing."

So why does he stay in the game when, in eleven years

working for his present employer, his per-mile rate has increased from thirty cents to thirty-six cents?

"What am I going to do? For me, I'm dilly-dallying here. For me, I make $5 a day and I'm happy. But I'm better off today than any driver because I'm making $35,000 a year with my company, and I average $55,000 a year with my pensions and everything. But the ordinary guy is a $35,000-a-year man. He's up against the wall. And every driver wants to make money. But since deregulation came in, you can't make money."

You can't make nearly as much money, to be sure. When Michael Belzer took a before-and-after glimpse at the deregulation of the U.S. trucking industry in his book *Sweatshops on Wheels*, he found that per-mile shipping rates plummeted 44 per cent between 1977 and 1987. Many have benefited from the lower cost of transporting goods. Manufacturers, wholesalers, and retailers have improved their bottom lines as a result, and some of the savings have been passed on to consumers.

But legions of trucking companies succumbed to the competitive pressures and went bankrupt. And drivers who wished to uphold their pre-deregulation standard of living had but one option in the face of lower per-mile payments: to drive faster and work longer.

The churn rate is estimated to be as high as 130 per cent, which means to fill 100 jobs, the average trucking company must hire 130 new drivers every year. To put that in perspective, at the height of the technological explosion in Silicon Valley, where Internet start-up firms paid

astronomical salaries and stock-option packages because
qualified workers were so scarce, the turnover rate was
about 20 per cent. And it's going to get worse. The size of
the white male population between 35 and 54 – currently
the biggest supplier of U.S. drivers – is expected to decline
by about 3 million Americans between 2004 and 2014.
According to a study commissioned by the American
Trucking Association, the supply of long-haul truckers is
expected to rise 1.6 per cent per year over those ten years.
But the demand will grow by 2.2 per cent. Some 219,000
drivers will need to replace the drivers aged fifty-five-plus
who will retire in the next decade, and that doesn't include
the drivers needed immediately to replace the drivers who
left the industry today and yesterday. As the report pointed
out, it partly comes down to money. Trucking-industry
wages declined during an economic downturn in 2000 and,
as of 2004, they had yet to recover. For instance, the 1990s
saw truck drivers earn average weekly wages that were 6 to
7 per cent higher than the average weekly wage in construction. But by 2001, truckers' wages were about 9 per cent
lower than those of construction workers. When once the
trucking industry could recruit new drivers from the ranks
of labourers who had maximized their earning potential
on the job site, the balance had tipped. As the American
Trucking Association report concluded, alleviating the
driver shortage will demand increasing wages.

But it's not simply a matter of bumping paycheques by
a few per cent. The report pointed out that companies
would do well to weigh the loss in productivity that might

result from designing schedules to ease the frustration that inevitably stems from the average driver's most common complaints: too much time away from home and the unpredictability of their return date.

Canada, so intertwined with the United States in matters of trade and trucking, has the same problems. A 2004 study commissioned by the Canadian Trucking Human Resources Council estimated that some 224,000 new truckers will be required between 2004 and 2010 to quench the demand fuelled by economic growth and attrition. That's about 37,000 new drivers a year.

The Canadian industry, as a result, has been pushing the federal government to relax immigration standards to allow for an influx of qualified foreign drivers, a suggested solution that hasn't been criticized as roundly as a 2001 call from the U.S. Truckload Carriers Association to lower the age limit for a commercial driver's license from the current twenty-one (which applies both in Canada and the United States) to eighteen. To old-timers, it was sacrilege, not to mention a safety hazard, to even consider unleashing a teenager at the wheel of an eighty-thousand-pound rig. Some pointed out that in years past, before competition came to its current head, big established companies wouldn't hire drivers under twenty-five. And some of them wouldn't hire drivers over twenty-five who hadn't apprenticed on the loading docks, moved trailers in the yard, and made the occasional local delivery. In arguing against lowering the age limit, the Owner-Operator Independent Drivers Association cited U.S. statistics that put the crash risk of automobile drivers aged 16 to 20 at almost twice that of drivers aged 21 to 24. Those types of numbers only strengthen the case of industry leaders keen to recruit experienced drivers from foreign shores.

"There isn't a week that goes by that I don't get phone calls from qualified drivers from Romania, Hungary, Poland, the U.K., even Australia and New Zealand, that would like to come here but they're not deemed to be skilled labour for the purposes of immigration," David Bradley, president of the Canadian Trucking Alliance, has said. "I think we have an intellectual snobbishness that's associated with our immigration policies. If you don't have a Ph.D. or a master's degree, it's very difficult to get in . . ."

One Winnipeg company found a way in. Desperately in need of experienced flatdeck drivers, the company sought out and successfully landed ten drivers from Britain and Germany. In the United States, an FBI sting operation uncovered a Tampa driving instructor who allegedly fixed tests for nine hundred immigrant drivers from Eastern Europe, some of whom lacked the basic English to read road signs. All of them were willing to work for rock-bottom wages.

There is compelling evidence to suggest that accident rates are linked to driver pay. J.B. Hunt Transport Services, an Arkansas-based behemoth, raised per-mile pay by about 38 per cent in 1996 – an experiment meant to reap benefits in both safety and driver retention – and cut its crash rate 50 per cent in a year. Another study found that for 10 per cent increase in compensation, a carrier will experience 9.2 per cent fewer crashes.

But progressive experiments in raising wages aren't exactly commonplace, and drivers have little power to influence the course of the business. About 25 per cent of drivers carry union cards, and though recent years have seen organized labour halt activity at seaports in Vancouver and Los Angeles, wreaking havoc on businesses near and far that relied on those dockyards as an entry point for myriad imports, from Australian wine to Chinese toys, those truckers represent a small percentage of the highway-driving populous.

"You have to understand that the typical driver out there is a loner," Gregory Miletti, a U.S. union driver, told the *U.S. News & World Report* in 2000. "Can you honestly see these last American cowboys getting up on a soapbox to voice their dissent? Not likely."

It has been estimated that U.S. truckers are putting in so many illegal hours that the industry would have to hire 130,000 more drivers – at a cost of $2 billion to $7 billion – to stay legal. The legal work week is 60 hours in the United States and *U.S. News & World Report* obtained a U.S. Department of Transportation (DOT) report that said truckers average 66 hours a week on the road, 75 hours if they don't belong to a union. Some 10 per cent of truckers are driving more than 100 hours a week.

As much as 25 per cent of drivers' time is spent waiting for loading and unloading. The sad joke is that, although it would seem logical that those long loading-dock waits could be used to catch much-needed shut-eye, truckers aren't generally free to sleep. They must be at the ready to respond to the whim of shipping and receiving. They must make that time up on the road, going faster, working longer.

"We think a sweatshop environment has developed, where the drivers have to work harder, not smarter," Michael Belzer, the Michigan economist, has said.

"Low wages and long hours may actually be the mortar that holds together the foundations of distribution and trade, and those conditions characterize both labor and management in trucking," wrote Belzer in *Sweatshops on Wheels*. "[Trucking companies] do not have the power to raise wages substantially because they are caught in a race to the bottom. . . . The problem therefore is more complex than a simple struggle between management and labour. The problem lies with public policy that supports unbridled competition in every sphere as a blanket solution to our social and economic problems."

Korny yawns a big yawn in the sun.

"Myself, when I'm tired, I lays down," he says. "I tell 'em, 'Hey, you can jump in the lake and I'll be there when I'll be there.' I was just talking to one of our boys yesterday, I was talking to one of our men that had to go down, 'a way down, into the States somewhere, I forgot where now. And I met him down in Monroe, Michigan. And I met him at eight o'clock in the morning, and he's been running since eight o'clock the morning before. He said, 'Man, I'm pooped, I'm going to bed.' I says, 'Sure, go to bed.'"

The parking lot buzzes all around us, the comings and goings of the rigs throwing up from the gravel clouds of dust that seem forever suspended above the fuel pumps. A moustachioed man in aviator sunglasses and snakeskin cowboy boots limps past us, and Korny greets him with a smile and a hello, the latter of which is reciprocated in a southern drawl. Two men follow close behind, both of them turbaned, both of them brown-skinned. Korny spots them, turns his body slightly to avoid their gaze, and lowers his voice.

"Then again," he says, "the worst part about trucking is here you've got two guys over here, and these guys will run your balls off. In the meantime, they're making it bad for the rest of the guys. [The company] will say to them, 'I want you to go, go, go.' And they'll just keep on going. They'll go, go, go, go. Whereas I, as a Canadian person, will say to the [dispatcher], 'Drop dead.' I always say to my dispatcher: 'Were you in bed last night sleeping? Good, eh? I was driving all night long.' Just like now, I was driving all night long, but I'm in good shape because I had a good rest."

In 2004, the United States Department of Homeland Security gave about $19 million to the American Trucking Association for the formation of a volunteer group of truckers, toll-booth collectors, and rest-stop attendants to work as what *Time* magazine called "terrorist hunters." A reporter for *Time* attended a training session for the so-called Highway Watch, wherein one Arkansas truck driver explained how he spots "Islamics." Turbans, the trucker told *Time*, are a telltale sign.

"I'll be honest: They know they're not welcome at truck stops. There's still a lot of animosity toward Islamics," said the trucker.

Said another Highway Watch member: "You can tell where they're from. You can hear their accents. They're not real clean people."

Ingrained racism, no matter how ill-informed its roots, isn't soon to be erased in the post-September 11 era, and CB chatter, especially in the southern United States, is often rife with hateful epithets when drivers with un-American accents pipe up. At a truck stop just up the highway from where I met Korny, I met Elvis Nelson, a twenty-four-year-old Canadian whose family hails from the Punjab, who was barely two years into his career as a produce hauler and who'd heard his share of slurs. Nelson was a rare character: He said the main reason he'd taken up trucking was to further his enjoyment of Internet courting. He was in the habit of seeking out cyber-savvy women in the area of his pending port of call, and it usually wasn't a problem, he said with a sly smile, to get them to venture to an appointed truck stop for an introductory cup of coffee.

His days on the road were numbered, he figured. The coming year would see him enter into an arranged marriage with an Indian woman he had yet to meet. He said he was "okay" with this tradition.

"It's cool. I've spoken to her on the phone," said Nelson, "and she doesn't want me to keep on trucking. She wants me to be at home."

Korny lifts the cap off his head and sighs.

"Yeah, trucking has gone all to rat shit. It's gone all to rat shit."

It was a gentler business when Korny was a younger man. The horsepower wasn't so intimidating. The company gave you twelve hours for the drive from Toronto to Windsor, a journey that now takes less than four hours. But on the old No. 2 highway, which boasted just one lane each way for long stretches and passed through main streets and stoplights, Korny remembers it taking him ten hours to make the trek. He tells of how truckers stopped to help stranded motorists and fellow truckers alike, how there was honour in their ranks, how the average person appreciated a trucker's worth.

In his words I hear echoes of others. Uwe Petroschke is a generation younger than Korny, but his experience is similar. An immigrant who came to Canada as a child in 1966, he worked his way up from the bottom of the trucking-company ladder. As a schoolboy he worked part-time at night, typing up shipping documents. He liked what he saw and kept at the business, striking out on his own, a single truck the backbone of his fledgling company. The fledgling company grew into a multi-million-dollar business. He has found a profitable niche in fragile cargo: computers and TVs and the like – anything that can't endure a pounding and must be specially packed to ensure safe transport.

In an unconventional decision, Petroschke put artwork on the side of his trucks, idyllic line-drawn images accompanied by a single word. "Surrender" was one of the messages, "Destiny" another. Stuck in traffic, had you pulled up next to one of Uwe's trucks, you might also have been asked to "Dream."

"I'm not marketing the company," he says. "I'm marketing an idea of putting something more beautiful on the roads. The trucking business has been good to me, and this is just one of the ways I could think of to give something back. I want people to feel good about trucking. These days we're one rung above used-car salesmen, or maybe we're one rung below."

Korny, back at the truck stop, shrugs a weary shoulder, a single palm pushing skyward.

"Now it's a world of go, go, go," he says. "We've got heavy highways. If you stop, you'll get in an accident. Everything's on the move, see what I mean. Cop'll give you a ticket if you stop. Back then it was a helpful world of trucking and men knew one another. You stopped at truck stops and you talked. Now nobody says two words to you some days."

I say, "You must be an exception to the rule."

"Hey, right now, I am better off than any sucker sitting on the twelfth floor of some apartment, dying slowly," he says. "I'm getting around. I meet people. My life is very full of going. Whereas, them other people, they're just dying slowly. But then again, a lot of elderly people, they get to that age, they want to be at that age. Well, if that's the way you want to do it, then dig your own grave slowly. Many, many of my friends, at my age, I've said, 'Hey, man, what have you got to lose? Come on with me for a week or two.

Pack up your suitcase.' And they'll say, 'Oh, I've got a dog here or a cat and I've got to look after the grass.' And I say, 'Oh, I've been talking to you twenty minutes too long. Goodbye, Johnny.' Nobody ever comes."

There is solace, though, in thinking about where his family came from and where it resides. Korny's parents were Russian immigrants who raised him in Montreal. His father was a sailor, doing hard labour on freighters for forty-some years. Korny was fifteen years old and big for his age when, in his youthful enthusiasm to join the Second World War, he doctored his driver's license to make himself appear eighteen. He joined the merchant navy, worked on supply ships at the conflict's tail end, and stayed a sailor on the Great Lakes until 1951, when he became a trucker.

And Korny's son, Thom, was, according to his father, a troubled teen. Thom found his legs on the water, joining the navy at his parents' request, emerging with the education that allowed him to become a computer engineer. He lives in Seattle.

"I was just up there visiting him," says Korny, "and that guy is wallowing in money. He's a top-notch computer fireman. He goes all over the world and sets up computers. He makes $125 an hour plus expenses paid. He's so computerized that he couldn't even talk to women. He wanted to date a girl that was all computer talk. And finally he met a lovely lady down in Halifax who was a pharmacist, so she talked a lot of computers. She was a pharmacist of $80,000, and she went further in her studies and now she's a doctor, an adviser to doctors on chemistry. Now she's a doctor of $160,000, and that's all American money. They did good and I'm glad for 'em.

"I'm glad because my boy was a navy man for nine years. The navy made a man out of him . . . We have a good rapport together. He said to me, 'Dad, I'm so glad you looked after me.' I'm just glad he didn't get into this business."

A stone's throw away, the rigs keep filing in for fuel and Korny is soon talking of the place his business is headed. The place is Mexico. And it turns out Korny's theory – that cheaper Mexican drivers will one day take jobs away from Canadians and Americans, all the while causing wages to diminish even further – has been widely espoused. When the original NAFTA agreement was signed in 1992, it included a stipulation that the U.S. border would be open to Mexican truck traffic in 2001. As of this printing, the border remains closed. And that's been as much a function of post-September 11 security concerns as deft lobbying. William Lipinski, an Illinois democrat in the U.S. House of Representatives, made a speech in 1999 that summed up the fears of many in the U.S. and Canadian trucking business.

"Does Mexico have logbooks? No," Lipinski said at the time. "Does Mexico have vehicle maintenance standards? No. Does Mexico have roadside inspections? No. Does Mexico have safety rating systems? No. Does Mexico have medical certification of drivers? No. Simply put, Mexico does not have any oversight of their trucking industry, yet they want the United States to allow their unregulated, unsafe Mexican trucks, which weigh up to 106,000 pounds, well over the U.S. limit of 80,000 pounds, to barrel down our highways and byways."

Lipinski also quoted some startling figures: that of the less than 1 per cent of Mexican trucks and Mexican drivers inspected at the border, over 40 per cent had failed inspections and been placed out of service; and that, according to a report by the U.S. Department of Transportation's inspector general, over 250 Mexican motor carriers had travelled illegally beyond the NAFTA border zone, a narrow band of free-access pavement that allows for the dropping off and picking up of freight by foreign carriers.

The case against an open U.S.–Mexico border, which could lead to a substantial increase in the amount of truck traffic, isn't merely economic. Pollution from NAFTA truck traffic is already making children who live near the border sick, according to a study by the Commission for Environmental Cooperation, a NAFTA agency. The study said that between 1997 and 2001, an average of about seven thousand children per year visited a hospital for breathing problems in the Mexican border city of Ciudad Juárez. There are "significant associations" between the particulate matter released by diesel trucks, among other machines, and child mortality.

One of the study's co-authors said that Mexico's air-quality standards require improvement, since despite the high rate of childhood respiratory problems – and despite the 696 children aged one month to a year who died during the five-year study, 231 of which died of causes related to

respiratory illness – Mexico's standard for dangerous ozone
levels was exceeded on only fourteen occasions.

"Children were being rushed to the hospital on days
when no air quality alarms were sounding," said Dr.
Matiana Ramírez Aguilar. "This suggests that lower levels
of ozone affect children's respiratory health."

Ramírez Aguilar said children may be more suscepti-
ble to particulate matter because they possess a reduced
capacity to metabolize toxic substances. But the traffic
keeps increasing. In 2001, more than 1 million trucks crossed
the border between Ciudad Juárez and El Paso, Texas. The
Mexican side of the border is a scarier place for the trans-
porters of goods.

Theft is a problem. In the mid-1990s, Kimberly-Clark,
the paper-products company, claimed that one of its trucks
was hijacked in Mexico nearly every day. The hijackers
would pose as Mexican police, complete with badges and
standard-issue clothing, force drivers to pull off the road,
then take the driver hostage, and make off with the goods.
The driver would soon turn up, unharmed, somewhere
down the road. The empty rig would emerge, not far from
the crime scene, a couple of days later.

These so-called *robos de carretera* were said by some to
be at "epidemic levels," and they most often involved high-
end shipments of computers, electronics, and clothes – the
kinds of goods easily moved from a market stall or a family
store. The Mexican government responded by increasing
the number of police on the roads. But the hijackers, who

seemed to know a truck's travel schedule and its contents, were rarely caught. Insurance premiums for trucking companies who do business in Mexico soared.

"Ahh, it's too bad," Korny says, "but trucking has gone all to rat shit."

As the resident chaplain in his trailer-turned-church in the parking lot of the Petro Truck Stop in Rochelle, Illinois, Jay LeRette gets less sleep than a deadline-pushing produce hauler. His fifty-three-foot house of worship is open 24-7. He's there six days a week. And so he steals a few winks when he can – which is whenever he isn't ministering one of two daily services or officiating at a wedding or a funeral for one of his flock of regulars, or when a trucker in need of ecclesiastical guidance isn't rapping on the door. On a slow day he'll get to bed after midnight. But almost inevitably these days he'll be roused to find at his door a weary trucker or, on rarer occasions, a prostitute, or, rarer still, an angry trucker wielding a gun.

Such was the wee-hours greeting on a rainy night a few years back, when LeRette – or Brother Jay, as he requests you call him – awoke to find a bearded man in a camouflage jacket threatening suicide and homicide as he confessed to a litany of sins. He said he'd failed as a father and a husband. He said he had a drug problem that was leaving his wife and family with an empty bank account and a hardscrabble existence.

"He was a Vietnam veteran and a trucker and he just started saying, 'Life ain't worth living! I'm mad!'" remembers LeRette. "He said he was going to kill himself, and when I started pressing in, he threatened to kill me, too."

Though LeRette has been a man of the cloth for more than a quarter century, this particular brush with danger wasn't exactly unprecedented. It was in the quiet hours of another late night, after all, that he came upon his current calling – this while serving a sentence in Illinois' LaSalle County Jail for a long list of adolescent transgressions that put him in the state's custody for most of his teenaged years and a good chunk of his early twenties. He was a thief and a fighter, mostly. He stole motorcycles because he loved to ride them. He fought in biker bars because he loved to start a melee.

The marks of his misspent youth are still with him, a tattoo on his left forearm bearing the letters LSD – "I did a lot of that stuff," he says of the street drug – and a five-centimetre scar on his cheek from the long-necked bottle of Budweiser that nearly removed his eye after he accepted an invitation to take an argument into an alley and was blindsided by a double-teaming enemy.

"I had good parents who loved me, and I went to a country school – when I look back it was a good school. I just had a rebellious streak inside me," he says. "By the age of thirteen I started getting locked up in detention homes. I had doctors and judges and psychiatrists and lawyers and state's attorneys and parole officers – they've all said, 'Mr. LeRette, you're unfit for society. You'll be a ward of the state of Illinois all of the days of your life.' And I really was a basket case. I stuttered all the time because of all the drugs and the drinking. You know how your body will twitch because of all the drugs? I was a mess."

He was a mess, he says, until that night at the county jail, when he began to flip through a pocket version of the New Testament in his one-man cell and, though he was neither raised a Christian nor had ever set foot in a church, "a light went on in my head and it all started to make sense." When he was released six months later, he hit Chicago's streets, carrying as he did an eight-foot cross while handing out leaflets and pocket Bibles and, when he gathered enough of a crowd, holding impromptu open-air revivals on the corner.

He preached in jails and in youth detention homes, sharing his venom-to-virtue tale. His stutter, he says, subsided. His yearning for trouble – for booze and for drugs – disappeared. And then, in 1990, he heard another Christian evangelist put out a call for truck-stop ministers. He contacted Transport for Christ International, which these days has ministers at thirty truck-stop chapels in North America, including four in Canada, and he found a home along Interstate 39. Transport for Christ isn't the only truck-wise ministry, but it's perhaps the most prominent. The early part of this decade has seen the organization expand to include three chapels in Moscow, with plans for additional outposts in Kenya and Tanzania.

It's a wider reach than was perhaps ever envisioned by Jim Keys, Transport for Christ's founder, the Canadian son of a truck driver who became a born-again Christian in 1950 and, by 1951, began visiting sick drivers in hospitals and preaching at the headquarters of the rare trucking companies that would allow him in the door. By 1968, Keys told his wife, Almeda, that he'd been compelled by God to build a chapel on an eighteen-wheeler, and that they'd need to sell their house to pay for it. But less than a decade later, with Transport for Christ's assets totalling some five hundred thousand dollars, Keys was quitting his mission, citing "religious politics" and founding the Association for Christian Truckers, which remains active.

Keys, who died in 1996, once said, "I've had a lot of smart-mouthed guys say to me, 'Hah! If I go to hell, I'll be with a lot of buddies.' No! You'll be alone. There's no buddying in hell."

There is no disputing the niche that truck-stop religion continues to fill. Although it's a predominantly Christian phenomenon in North America, there are North American–style truck stops that serve at least one other religion. On the road to Kuala Lumpur, Malaysia, for instance, there is a famed rest stop that's suspended over the highway that, along with the KFC and A&W fast-food kiosks, features a Muslim prayer room that is said to accommodate some 1,000 people every day.

Howard E. Jones, the former president of Transport for Christ, has said, "In this world, we're in Satan's backyard. And when you're in trucking, you're right in the sandbox . . . There are all kinds of temptations for truckers – sex and drugs and pornography. They're away from the home four to six weeks at a time. He gets a call while he's on the road – his kid was hit by a car, his daughter's run away with some motorcyclist. This fellow's two thousand miles from home. He's distraught. He's really not in a position to drive an [eighty-thousand]-pound rig."

LeRette's work isn't without its frustrations. There are those who have a hard time reaching out to him, such as the burly veteran driver who confessed to being ashamed to walk into the chapel in broad daylight for fear of being seen by his colleagues.

"I never imagined these guys have their own kind of peer pressure, but it's true," says the chaplain. "Some guys actually wait until it gets dark to come in and see me. I had one guy, went by the name of Big Daddy, he came in one night and said he had some problems. He was from Texas, from the wrong side of the tracks, and he said he had people on one side of his street who wanted him to haul marijuana, and he had people on the other side of his street who wanted him to haul cocaine. He said, 'I could make good money, but I don't want to keep living this kind of a life.' But he said he'd been waiting in his truck for hours, until it got dark, and that he'd actually driven fifty miles down the freeway – this is what he said – and turned around before he could muster the courage to come into the chapel."

There are those LeRette cannot reach, such as the father who brought his sixteen-year-old daughter and his wife to the truck stop and proceeded to prostitute them.

"I tried talking to them," he says. "I was just shocked. But as far as I know, they never did give their life to the Lord, and they stopped coming here."

He doesn't necessarily wait for people to come to him. He announces services on the truck-stop public-address system, and sometimes he'll roam the parking lot, his eight-foot cross in tow, drumming up disciples.

"The drivers are gone so long away from their wives and their churches and their families. Some drivers are gone a week, two weeks, even a couple of months at a time. And there's really no accountability out there on the road," he says. "They get involved in drugs and drinking and gambling, and they lose a lot of money, and they're not able to take any money home to pay the bills."

But neither does he limit his missionary work to the truck stop. He's an avid rider of horses, and he'll often fill his saddlebags and set out from his rural homestead to spread the word in the centres of nearby towns. He still rides a motorcycle – an old Harley-Davidson he purchased a while back – and that passion has granted him entrance into the clubhouses of various biker gangs.

"The truck drivers, the bikers, and the cowboys, for whatever reason, they kinda like each other. They can [empathize] with each other. I don't know if it's because they've got the same mentality or what. But yes, the bikers, the truckers, and cowboys get along well," he says. "I don't see a lot of salvations in the biker ministry. But I do see an example every now and then. They'll be standing there with their buddies, tattoos and long hair and a knife on their side, and you'll begin to talk to them and you begin to penetrate 'em, start to pierce their heart. And all of a sudden, maybe even a tear will start to well up in their eye, and they'll say, 'All right, preacher, stop it. You're getting through. Thank you for being here, but not now. Back off.'"

His evangelism has been repelled with more than words. He's been spit on. He's been swung at. He's been cursed. But he has only been threatened at gunpoint on that rainy night a few years back. As that tense moment wore on, LeRette remembers the trucker's story getting worse, the trucker getting more agitated. His wife, it turns out, had just left him for his best friend. He had debts he couldn't pay. The situation looked bleak for the trucker and for the preacher.

"I'll be honest. I know the Bible says we shouldn't be filled with fear, but I was," LeRette says. "This guy was a lot bigger than me, and I know I couldn't have got by him (to reach the door). I started thinking about making a new door in the wall. I began to back off, and I said, 'Sir, there was a time in my life when I really thought life wasn't worth living. There was a time when I literally wanted to take my own life.' I said, 'I know you've made a lot of mistakes in your life, but I believe right now can be a turning point to begin to surrender your life to Christ and ask for forgiveness.' And through the grace of God I was able to get him calmed down. The same man who wanted to kill me ended up giving me a big hug, saying, 'Thank you, preacher. Thank you for being here.'"

Truckers are the rugged individualists of the working class. They all share some things in common, but there are countless variations on the theme. There are the owner-operators of shiny chrome tankers, the kind who haul poisonous solvents or skim milk. There are the hardy devotees of the flatbed, the bane of whose existence is that almost everything they haul needs to be secured with a bevy of straps and tarps that need to be applied in all weather.

The sporting world, where I often tap the laptop, is more conformist by comparison. One jock got a tattoo and now an extensive ink collection seems to be a job requirement of the athletically inclined. Locker rooms don't generally tolerate the sore thumb. It's easier to fall in line than stand out. But there are exceptions, and one of them is Karl Malone. Malone, when he played in the National Basketball Association from 1986 to 2004, was unique for more than one reason. He hailed from a state, Louisiana, that's never been a basketball factory. He attended a relatively small university, Louisiana Tech, that has produced exactly four other NBA players since 1961. And for all the under-the-breath buzz that he was a hayseed and a simpleton – a first impression that was formulated when Malone showed up at the NBA draft in an outfit for the ages, featuring a cloth necktie that hung from his Adam's apple and ended abruptly around his sternum – the man had ideas. In an era in which much of the conventional wisdom suggested lifting weights couldn't help the purveyors of a finesse game like basketball, he lifted weights like the most faithful practitioner of a fundamentalist religion, building his six-foot-nine-inch frame into a spectacle of marble-hard muscularity. At a time when the majority of his colleagues prided themselves on their Armani suits and their alligator shoes, Malone often wore a plaid shirt and jeans and cowboy boots to his arena-workplace. He had bodybuilder biceps when the game's best coaches were convinced such bulky appendages would put his finesse game in a funk. Instead of joining the fraternity, he seemed to pay no attention to the ways of others. In staying true to his beliefs and his theories, he became something of a pioneer. He's known as the greatest power forward to ever play the game. He's responsible for the shift in thinking that turned basketball players from skinny beanpoles to ripped behemoths. He's a groundbreaker.

But for all the weight he threw around, he influenced nary a colleague when it came to his off-season pastimes. For a lot of years, after all, Malone spent the summer months working as a long-haul trucker, driving his Freightliner across the continent. This is a man, after all, who made multi-millions at his day job, $2.5 million a year in 1992. But the purpose of his truck-driving sideline wasn't merely recreational. The cargo was real – in the summer of 1993, for instance, he did a regular run of Idaho potatoes from Idaho Falls to Layton, Utah, not to mention a haul of frozen products from Salt Lake City to Shreveport, Louisiana – and so was the reaction from the folks he met at truck stops along the route.

"They loved it that somebody like Karl Malone would be doing what they do," Malone would say years later, speaking in a locker room in Toronto. "I did it because it was a love of mine; it's still a love of mine. I love to drive, I just love to get away. I also respect what truckers do . . . And also, you get to see another part of a guy's profession. I've always said that truckers remind me of cargo ships. I don't think [truckers] realize how important they are to our society.

"I've always said, if truckers want to get their message across, stop wherever you're at for five hours one day. Wherever you're at, just stop right there for five hours. And all these gas prices, all these taxes, they'd start going the other way. It's not that you're trying to smear it in somebody's face, it's just you don't feel like things are right and you need to do something about it."

Malone, as much as he was a star, was also a working man's basketballer. His was a slow rise to dominance, fuelled by work ethic as much as genetic predisposition. They called him The Mailman, because he delivered. He won a gold medal as a member of perhaps the greatest roster ever assembled, the so-called Dream Team that included Michael Jordan, Magic Johnson, and Larry Bird, among others. But Malone was never solely obsessed by roundball excellence. He grew up in the small town of Summerfield, Louisiana, where his grandmother owned a store. As a boy he'd see the truckers roll into town and covet their lot in life.

"I've dreamed of this ever since I was a little kid," said Malone in 1992, discussing his budding trucking concern, Malone Enterprises. "I love trucks. On the road, it's just me and the machine. People expect me to wear jewellery, suits, and drive a Mercedes. But I love cowboy boots, jeans, country music, and trucks. These are the things that make me tick."

Indeed, one of Malone's first orders of business when he decided to expand his company from a lone truck to a fleet of as many as five Freightliners was to paint the trailers with cowboy scenes. He's been a cattle farmer, too.

He also considers himself a logger, and he formed a company to harvest tracts of timber for some of North America's largest logging companies to prove it. Loggers need truckers, of course, and Malone, for a lot of reasons, needed both callings in his life, although he acknowledged that neither off-season pastime would have been possible without his basketball player's bankroll. But he got out of the trucking business, learning first-hand the frustrations facing workaday drivers and fleet owners.

"Take the basketball player away from it – it's tough to make a go at it," he said. "My thing is, it's kinda like anything else. Back in the old days, the more you worked, the more you were rewarded, the nicer your cheque was. Now, the more you work, the longer the hours – it's $50 here, $75 here, $30 here – they're taking for this new law, this new law, this new law. You know, it used to be people would say, 'That's what I want to do. I want to drive truck for a living.' Now you see all the rules and regulations they're putting on you, people don't want to do that no more. Because it's not, 'I'm just going to go out and work and I'm going to get this.' Nowadays it's like, you go out and earn more and they want to take more."

2

The Ultimate Fan

One of the things that infuriates Devi, a trucker with a healthy disdain for the not-so-endearing habits of most other truckers, is that truck-stop hygiene is, to her eyes and nose, an oxymoron. Another thing that raises her ire is that the last time she used the word *oxymoron* in what had otherwise been a conversation of rare reason on the CB, her suddenly angry colleague shouted her down for likening him to the offspring of a beast of burden and a dimwit.

"I'm not kidding – he thought I was calling him a cross between an ox and a moron," she says. "It's like, some days I can't believe I'm a truck driver. I just sort of am. I may drive a truck for a living, but I don't call myself a truck driver. I actually call myself an international freight relocation technician. I tell everybody that – even truck drivers. I say, 'Truck drivers are a disgrace.' They say, 'You're a truck driver, too.' And I say, 'No, I'm not. I'm an international freight relocation technician.' And they just split a gut. Everybody in the trucking industry gets a total kick out of that."

In more than fifteen years as a slim minority in a male-dominated vocation, Devi – whose given name rhymes with Chevy – has developed plenty of techniques to navigate the potholes and the men attached to the pot bellies that are among her occupational hazards. If you're a woman driving solo – let alone a young and physically fit woman with spiky platinum hair, tattoos, two gold loops in each earlobe, and three gold necklaces – there are sociological obstacles standing in the way of your career contentment. Industry estimates suggest just 5 per cent of long-haul drivers, after all, are women, and many of those women qualify as the better half of a husband-wife driving team. But perhaps most daunting, there is, at every stop along your perpetual journey, a gauntlet of lonely men standing between you and the bathroom.

"I walk through truck stops with my head down. I lift my eyes just enough so I can see where I'm walking. I don't look at anybody. I don't smile at anybody. I don't talk to anybody. And a lot of people that walk by go, 'You'd look a lot better with a smile on your face.' And I'll look up and I'll smile and I'll keep going. But I don't want to attract attention.

"As soon as you look them in the eye, that starts a conversation," she says. "And a conversation leads to aggravation."

Devi's aggravation at this moment is a silver Toyota sedan that is weaving its haughty nose through near-imperceptible gaps in the traffic on this crowded Texas highway. The little import has just sliced from the far-left lane to within an arm's length of the bumper of Devi's Eagle 758, a burping monster more than forty times the Toyota's weight. Her truck's cab is painted a deep burgundy, its fifty-three-foot trailer a stock mud-splattered white. Checking her mirrors, one to her left that allows her to see down the length of her leviathan, the other out the passenger window that gives her a view of the shoulder, she suddenly slaps the wheel in astonishment, shaking her head and shrugging. She reaches up for the handle of her air horn, which hangs near the upper left corner of the windshield if you're on the inside looking out, but she refrains from registering her complaint publicly and opts instead for the international gesture of incredulity: Two raised palms and a dropped jaw.

She is driving on the outskirts of Dallas in the scrolling dusk, but she's seen this stunt in the contiguous forty-eight states and ten provinces.

"These four-wheelers, they slam on the brakes right in front of you. Now, what kind of person has the brain capacity to slam on the brakes in front of a truck that's ten times their size?" she says. "They're in a Mazda Miata or a Honda or a Toyota. I'm an eighty-thousand-pound truck. Who's going to win? Who is going to win?"

There is no victory in highway calamity, so Devi rides her brakes and widens the gap between the Toyota and disaster. Hurrying, on this evening, is unnecessary, since the load of peat moss in her trailer isn't due at its intended port until morning. Tonight's destination is a hotel with truck parking where her passenger will rent a room while she spends the night in her bunk. I have been on board for less than an hour. Although we'd become acquainted in a lengthy back-and-forth on our respective phone-messaging systems, Devi and I had met up only that day in the parking lot of Dallas's Valleyview Mall. I had employed the services of Cowboy Cab to drive me to the mall from the airport, where I had arrived after a ridiculously circuitous sampling of runways in Houston, Jackson, Baltimore, and Buffalo. Discount airline tickets have a price, and in this case it's a sore back.

Less than two hours after I arrived, stooped, at the mall – after beginning an immersion in Dallas culture that included a long gaze at the window of a T-shirt shop ("Don't Mess With Texas" appears to be the state threat) and food-court sushi served by a woman who, in the midst of preparing my order, answered a cellphone that was sheathed in a plush stuffed duck – I got a call on my cellphone from Devi, who told me she was arriving in the parking lot. There we shook hands and said our hellos before she introduced me to her trusty companion Posh, a Chinese Shar-Pei or, to the layman, a brown wrinkle dog. The pooch promptly scaled my blue jeans and pawed my windbreaker before repairing to a lonely strip of grass in the sea of pavement to pee and preen.

Devi, who's been on the road for most of the last fifteen of her thirty-four years, was wearing a leather and felt jacket that bore the logo of Winnipeg Motor Express, the company for which she'd been hauling for the past few years. She's a company driver, which means the company supplies her with the truck, the trailer, and the loads. She is paid to drive by the mile.

When she picked me up, she was nearing the end of the southward leg of her journey. She expected that by early tomorrow afternoon, after her morning drop-off of the peat moss in nearby Troup, Tex., she would be reloaded with a shipment bound for the Canadian side of the border. She couldn't be sure of where she'd be headed – Toronto, maybe, or Calgary or Winnipeg – but she'd done this Texas run before and it was usually enviable in its out-and-back efficiency. And so we were off to the hotel, a light mist on the windshield requiring attention from the intermittent wipers, the glow of brake lights bathing the cab in warm pink light.

Her mailing address is a condominium in Winnipeg, but her home – the place she spends perhaps three hundred nights a year – is her truck. It's outfitted with relatively few conveniences, a TV but no satellite dish, a small plug-in cooler but no full-fledged fridge. She rarely eats without use of a can opener. "At least you know it's not going to go bad – canned peaches and pears and grapefruit," she says. "Cold beans are delicious."

The interior cargo space just behind us, what isn't taken up by Posh's welcome-mat-sized corduroy sleeping pad, is loaded with fitness equipment. There's a stair climber folded beneath the bottom-most of two bunks, and there's a pair of ten-pound dumbbells tucked in the corner beneath a pile of bedding. Devi, with her left hand on the wheel and her right hand employed as the evening's tour guide, points to the weights, to the cans of dog food under the bunk, and to the scattered stuffed animals, a beaver, a squirrel, an octopus.

Hers is the standard living area for the typical trucker; there are nicer abodes on the market. Big bunks, as they're known in the industry's jargon, add a few feet to the average behind-the-seat space. They're sold with washroom facilities, showers, and toilets, and they're also often outfitted with kitchens. They come with convection ovens and sinks and mini-fridges. It's a recreational vehicle for commercial use. And while they're heavier – and because of that less fuel efficient – manufacturers make compelling arguments for their economy in the long run. It's not uncommon to spend an hour waiting for a shower to come free in a travel plaza, and here's a shower available at one's whim. It's not cheap finding decent meals at North America's roadsides, and here's a kitchen that allows a health-conscious coupon clipper to eat cheaply and healthily along the way.

Devi, happy in her space, laughs at the clutter.

"There are projectiles in here. You don't want to have an accident – the TV might hit you in the head. The accident might not kill you, but the stuff in your house is going to."

Truck accidents, of course, are what a lot of folks worry about. But every truck-bound businessman knows one of the industry's mantras: "The cheap truck always runs." Since the United States deregulated the industry, rates have plummeted, bankruptcies have increased while wages have stayed the same. Canada deregulated its trucking industry in 1988, but Canadian truckers, some 80 per cent of whom earn part of their living in the United States, are inextricably linked to the U.S. system. Previous to deregulation there were regulatory hurdles for a company from one country that aimed to do business in the other country, so much of the freight was exchanged at the border and many truckers never touched rubber on foreign soil.

But deregulation and free trade changed all of that. According to Daniel Madar's book *Heavy Traffic: Deregulation, Trade and Transformation in North American Trucking,* Canadian revenues from transborder truck trade increased 148 per cent while transborder tonnage more than doubled between 1989 and 1997. Canadian motor carriers earned 74.6 per cent of their revenues domestically in 1988, a number that fell to 64.1 per cent in 1995. As a Statistics Canada report noted, free trade spurred "a reorientation of trucking activity from east-west to north-south."

What's going over? The most common commodity hauled to or from the United States is listed by Statistics Canada as "miscellaneous transported products." No. 2 on the list is "road motor vehicles, parts and accessories."

But while many companies have prospered, drivers haven't necessarily shared the wealth. Deregulation brought a sea change to the highways. As Belzer argued in *Sweatshops on Wheels*, "The only option left for individual drivers who are trying to maintain their standard of living [has been] to increase earnings by driving faster and working more hours." Investigative reporters, both on TV and in newspapers, have shone a light on the ever-present danger of tired truckers who breach the allowable limits of legal driving time in that pursuit. More truckers die in accidents each year than workers in any other profession. And though large trucks account for 4 per cent of all registered vehicles in the United States – and 7 per cent of total vehicle miles travelled – they were, in 2001, involved in 12 per cent of U.S. crashes. Canadian numbers tend to parallel the U.S. trends.

"Until you change the economics of trucking, nothing will happen," Bob McEvoy, a former director with the U.S. Federal Motor Carrier Safety Administration, has said.

The economics go like so. The average trucker works more than 3,000 hours a year by some counts. Most blue-collar workers in North America log about 2,000 hours a year. Since 1980, when Jimmy Carter's government stopped regulating rates and route structures, profit margins have narrowed and the median earnings of long-haul drivers have shrunk 30 per cent. Non-union long-haulers typically work about 70 hours per week – 10 hours more than the legal limit – for the equivalent of $8 per hour. In 2000, a trucker told *U.S. News & World Report* that she'd made $40,000 in 1999. "Truthfully," she said, "I didn't do it legally." The forty-one-year-old woman from Texas said she often worked eighty or ninety hours a week. According to a University of Michigan survey, nearly 56 per cent of drivers say they worked more hours than they logged in the previous thirty days.

In 1997, speeding truckers caused 253 fatal crashes involving other vehicles. Four-wheelers cause most fatal accidents with trucks, as many as 80 per cent according to an American Automobile Association survey. But in more than a quarter of those accidents, the truck driver is cited in police reports for making at least one error. Evidence suggests truckers are running longer and harder all the time. The average used truck sold in 2003 had 300,000-some miles on it. In 2005, that number was up to about 500,000 miles.

One of the key problems in policing any given trucker's penchant for driving longer-than-legal hours is the inherent weakness of the record-keeping system itself. Drivers on both sides of the border are required to record their daily goings-on in paper logbooks that are variously and derisively known as "lie books" and "comic books" and "cheat sheets." Law-enforcement types acknowledge that logbooks are ripe for exploitation, and few officers on either side of the border relish taking out a calculator and attempting to outsmart the trucker at his own game by attempting to prove fraudulent his creative accounting. The problem is it's an honour system with no honour. Lawrence J. Ouellet, in his 1994 book *Pedal to the Metal: The Work Lives of Truckers*, summed up the limitations of logbooks, and the law, in one memorable passage.

"I pull into a state weigh station, my logbook in my lap. I'm good at this now. If they signal me for an inspection, I'll have it updated by the time I stop. If they don't pull me in, I'll have more latitude in filling it out to make my work hours appear legal. I don't feel guilty. When they determined these limitations on hours, were drivers driving the comfortable rigs and good roads we have now? And don't human biorhythms matter? . . . Many times over the years I have been dangerously tired despite being within legal limits on my work hours, or absolutely alert though in violation of the law. If they were really serious about limiting driving time, it could be done . . . No, I don't feel guilty; I feel sharp."

The mockery that is the paper logbook might not be long for this world. Technology has existed for years that can electronically track the wheres and hows and how longs of a trucker's daily grind. Proponents of electronic on-board recorders – devices sometimes likened to the black boxes on aircraft that can track a truck's every movement – have long argued that mandatory installation of the devices would drastically reduce abuse of work limits. In 2005, the United States government dropped a proposal to bring the recorders into widespread use despite the support of some of the industry's major players, but their eventual implementation is thought by many to be inevitable.

"Keeping paper logbooks in this day and age is just stupid," one trucking executive told an industry meeting quoted in *Traffic World* magazine. "We need to go to on-board recorders to move the industry into the twenty-first century."

Up ahead is a sign for a hotel with the magic words – "Truck Parking" – towering over an expanse of puddled blacktop. I run into the lobby to check out the deal: It's thirty-five dollars a night with a continental breakfast – a steal, I figure – so I stick my head back out the door, give Devi the thumbs-up, and check in. Devi asks if she can borrow my shower – if I wasn't tagging along, after all, she'd be unwinding beneath a spout of warm water at the truck stop – so I go for a walk in the drizzle while she uses the room, happening upon a nearby gas station where I buy some snacks and inquire, too, about the availability of cold beer.

"This is a dry county," says the weathered attendant, unimpressed with my request. "You'd have to drive 'bout twenty miles."

I make do with a bottle of water and pretzels. Back at the hotel, Devi has one last request before she returns to her parking-lot quarters. She wants to borrow my laptop to log on to the Internet dating service in which she's recently enrolled. I oblige and offer to leave the room so she can troll for companionship in private. But she won't have any of it, and as she sits cross-legged on the shiny polyester bedspread with the earth-toned geometric pattern, she offers a commentary as she calls up the site and checks her messages.

"The last thing I want to do is date a truck driver," she says. "But there's an awful lot of truck drivers on this site, because truck drivers are constantly looking for somebody to date. I've been on [the site] about six weeks, and when I first started, I didn't want to tell anybody I was a truck driver. But the first guy I started talking to on the phone, I thought, I better tell him right away. So I said, 'I drive a truck for a living.' And he paused. And I thought, 'This is the reaction I thought I'd be getting.' And he said, 'Well, that's really shitty because so do I.' Which is not a good thing, because if I'm not around, he's not around . . .

"I said, 'Well, we can meet. Let's talk a few times.' His name was Fred. After a couple of meetings, it was like, 'So we drive trucks for a living. We have nothing else in common whatsoever.' I come from this Jewish middle-class family, and I was brought up in a very, very good area of Winnipeg – River Heights. And that was that."

She didn't aspire to be a highway-hugging wanderer. Trucker, after all, seemed a counterintuitive career choice for a lifelong lover of animals, a keeper of dogs and ducks, snakes and horses. She once had a pair of pythons named Snoopy and Woodstock; Snoopy died of asthma and Woodstock died because, for reasons never known, he suddenly quit eating. She had show dogs, but they weren't poofy poodles; they were Rottweilers. And back in 1988, after dropping out of high school against the counsel of her vice principal – "He said, 'You're ruining your life'" – she was fulfilling a childhood dream by working in the back stretch of a horse-racing track in Winnipeg, tending to the thoroughbreds and standardbreds. She was twenty-one. She was living with a man named Luke, a boyfriend a decade her senior.

Around that time Luke's sister announced her intention to become a trucker. Devi, already a little tired of the horse game's low wages, figured "Why not?" No matter that she had never even driven a car with a standard transmission.

She hopped in a truck and, in her words, "winged it." Two weeks later, after passing the test for her licence, she was on the road as half of a driver team, her boyfriend Luke doing most of the driving.

But the partnership lasted all of six months. "We were going to kill each other," she says. "You can't have two strong personalities. You can't have two bosses in the truck."

To keep the relationship together, they both quit driving. She worked as a dispatcher for sixteen months. But her love for the road outlasted their love. When she and Luke parted ways, she promptly hopped back into the cab, where she's been ever since.

After tapping away at the keys and chatting some more, she logs off the Internet and sighs.

"I'm actually pursuing a guy right now, and the guy I'm trying to pursue, it's quite obvious he's got plenty of money. And my friend Elena said, if it got to the point, would you quit driving? And I don't know if I could ever quit driving. She said, 'Well, you could drive in the city.' But to be confined in that city? I said to her, this is my compromise: I'll only drive 11,000 miles a month instead of 13,500 or 14,000, which is what I do now. And truck drivers will find that funny, because for some drivers 11,000 miles is a huge month.

"I mean, I was dating one guy, like, ten years ago, and he said, I'll build you a house and you can raise dogs and horses and you don't have to drive. And my mother said to me, 'If you allow somebody to decide what your future is going to be like – even though it sounds like a pretty grand future – you're going to resent him. And even if you want to go back on the road, you made this deal and you've got to stay in the city. You can't go back on the road. You have to know that that's what you want to do. And I don't think that's what you want to do.' My God, if I ever had done that back then, we would be divorced."

The next morning, after I indulge in the motel's complimentary continental breakfast (which, in this part of the world and, more to the point, in this price range, amounts to surprisingly decent coffee and a downright excellent granola bar), Devi steers her rig onto Route 53 with notable skill. Her skill is notable because, while she weaves her hulking machine through not-inconsiderable traffic, she is also balancing a road atlas on her lap while spooning Mini-Wheats and milk from a blue plastic cup.

"I always feel like I'm in a hurry," she says. "To me, eating outside the truck is a waste of time."

Saving time is the trucker's raison d'être, so multi-tasking is an alarming reality. Drivers fool with the squelch knob on their CBS – which allows them to block out or boost weak signals to reduce or increase the range of transmission – dial and answer cellphones, read transmissions on Qualcomm satellite dispatching systems. They evacuate. They sing. They feed dogs. They write songs. Back in 2003, one trucker from Ohio crashed his rig while attempting to change his clothes at 60 mph. He misjudged a curve and rolled off U.S. 6 in Indiana, where he was found naked by police. Nothing was bruised but his ego. The trucker reportedly said he had set his cruise control, a device that regulates the truck's speed. But cruise control is not to be confused with autopilot, which isn't yet an option on the rigs of this world. (Although there do exist computer-controlled systems that have yet to come into popular usage that maintain a strict following distance and keep a vehicle in the middle of its chosen lane.) Still, judging from the tales one hears at your average trucker's haunt, changing clothes at the wheel has certainly been successfully achieved more often than not.

Devi is slurping up the last of her cereal and drives past a billboard framed by dangling power lines: GUN SHOW, it blares. We pass Robert E. Lee High School, where the students are wearing headphones and toting backpacks on wheels and beginning to assemble. We pass Black C Baptist Church and a sign staked into scraggly grass: "Fear Not Tomorrow. God Is Already There." Though we're only fifteen minutes into our morning's journey, it isn't long before Devi begins to express indecision in her bearing, which seems to unnerve Posh, who whimpers as Devi glances at the map on her lap. It turns out she's been confused by the existence of two different roads known by the number 110. Slowing to let some traffic pass, she uses every inch of a four-lane road to execute a 180-degree change in direction.

"That's what you call a shit hook. It's a hook, and if the cops see you, you're in shit."

The difficulty of righting an erroneously navigated rig

shouldn't be understated. There's a song, "Give Me 40 Acres," in which the singer tells of his eternal troubles with reversing course without the luxury of forty acres of countryside. Devi, who can turn it on a dime, has no need for a tract of open field to test her turning radius. Finding the right route, she rolls under the sky's low ceiling until, a half-hour later, the destination appears. Parsley Farms, a greenhouse operation, is a mud pit. A man in a green cap bearing the logo of The Masters golf tournament meets us in the bog. He tells Devi to be careful not to get stuck, since he's already spent a day this week pulling another delivery truck out of a quagmire with a bulldozer. She slowly turns her truck as per the man's instructions, heeding the warning about venturing too deeply into the soft parts of the yard.

In a few moments, the man in the Masters cap has mounted an orange forklift with which he quickly begins to remove the cargo from Devi's truck, dropping the ten-foot-high pallets of peat moss wrapped in thick black plastic in neat rows. As he works, Devi takes Posh for a pee and a stroll. It's 9:15 a.m. and it's drizzling. Thirty minutes later, with the cargo emptied and the paperwork signed, we're back in the truck, waiting for word of another assignment from Devi's dispatcher. To pass the time, she shows me her tattoo.

To do this, she lifts the right sleeve of her T-shirt. I see that her shoulder is engulfed by the face of a famous man in a cowboy hat. The man is Garth Brooks, the country singer, and his head-and-shoulders incarnation measures perhaps eight inches high and five inches wide.

Devi says she is Brooks's most ardent fan, and although it's impossible to measure that claim, her credentials are impressive. She once paid a scalper $1,200 to see his show at the Great Western Forum in Los Angeles (even though Garth, she says, is morally opposed to ticket brokering). She's seen him in Minneapolis twice, in Fargo three times, in Sioux Falls four times. She's not the only trucker whose passion has been facilitated by far-flung assignments. Jim Cabage is a Tennessee trucker who has danced at more than 450 Jazzercise locations in forty-seven states and two provinces. He says he sees a man once every six classes.

Devi, for her part, has seen Garth thirteen times, enough that at least one of her former boyfriends has expressed his jealousy.

"It was unbelievable. We almost broke up over that," she says. "He thought I was nuts, and he was just a jealous nutcase himself."

In 1996, Devi made a publicity stunt out of her desire to meet her hero, erecting in the parking lot of a Winnipeg shopping mall a banner that read: "Garth Brooks: Your Ultimate Fan Wants to Meet You." Showing plenty of public relations savvy, she turned the stunt into a charity event – soliciting donations of cash and canned food on behalf of a local food bank. The local media offered daily updates on her progress.

The ultimate fan, though, never did meet Garth Brooks. The singer's three-night stand at Winnipeg Arena coincided with the nuptials of Devi's brother. She went to the Friday show, flew to Toronto on Saturday morning, attended the wedding, and returned to the prairie in time for the Sunday show. Brooks's people, aware of the banner in the shopping-mall parking lot but unaware of the wedding in Toronto, had planned on introducing her to the singer Saturday night. For whatever reason, there was no flexibility on this matter. The *Winnipeg Free Press* rubbed Devi's face in the unfortunate timing; "Brooks fanatic blows big chance" went the smirking headline.

Devi's only consolation was the knowledge that her kerfuffle raised three thousand pounds of food and nine hundred dollars, and that Garth thought enough of her efforts to leave behind a souvenir: an autographed acoustic guitar that is now housed in a custom acrylic case in Devi's condo.

"I think half of Winnipeg laughed at me and went, 'This is never going to happen.' Who's laughing now? Nice guitar I have, isn't it?" she says. "I like being who I am. I wish sometimes I wasn't so hyperactive. I tire myself out."

She puts her left hand over Garth's face and squeezes her shoulder.

"It's permanent proof of my temporary insanity. Everybody who gets a tattoo has temporary insanity. Why else would you want to deface your body like that – something so clean and mark it up," she says, wrinkling her nose. "They say, 'Well, it's personal expression.' But personal expression is having a little flower on your ass that nobody ever sees and you and your husband get a kick out of it. But when you go eight inches by five inches, that's an extreme measure of your personal expression."

Not all of her personal expression is as difficult to remove. Devi wears a gold ring that says GARTH on the middle finger of her right hand. Her left pinkie is adorned with a diamond-studded horseshoe. Her truck, although it belongs to her employer, is customized with body art of its own – custom decals. On the driver's door, just below the window, are the words: "Devil With Wings." (The letters are inch-high and white; the i's are dotted with hearts; the "Devil" is her nickname.) On the bottom of the driver's window: "Good Girl." (The o's are topped with a halo spiked with horns, a play on religious imagery that was once condemned by a passing CB evangelist whose handle was The Preacher.)

The back side of her sleeper is also customized with a memorial to the victims of September 11. There is a silhouette of the two towers and the words: "Some Gave All Now All Give Some: 11th September 2001."

And on the passenger door, just below the window, there is yet another label. It reads: "Reserved for # 9."

The "# 9," Devi explains, has recently replaced the name of Boyfriend #8, a truck driver named Billy with whom she broke up six months ago, before Billy actually sat in the passenger seat.

"Poor Billy. He was not a truck driver truck driver – he'd have two showers a day, brush his teeth three times a day at least," she says. "And he was extremely polite to customers; not a traditional truck driver at all. Took pride in his truck and his job."

Her voice trails off. Posh, sleeping somewhere behind

her, registers a dreamy moan. Devi, suddenly back on the job, picks up the Qualcomm – a satellite-linked computer the size of a thick hardcover book with which she communicates with the home office – and looks at its blank screen. Qualcomm, the U.S. company that is the industry leader in satellite tracking, monitors about three hundred thousand trucks at any given time.

"Nothing yet," she says.

Just then a muddied pickup truck pulls into the driveway in front of us. A man in blue jeans and a red ball cap approaches the driver-side window. He is one of the proprietors of Parsley Farms, a tall handsome Texan wearing cowboy boots and a saucer-sized belt buckle. Devi seems to know him. She gets out of the truck, and they begin to pace the lot together, walking and talking and laughing.

Ten minutes later, she is pulling herself back into her seat, consoling the farmer with an encouraging word.

"Don't give up hope," she says, and now the farmer has said his goodbyes and is walking away. "I'm thirty-four and single, and I still think there's someone out there for me."

She turns to me and explains, "He's going through a divorce. I thought he was going to start crying right there on the spot."

The drizzle has ceased and the humid air is getting warmer; the morning is slipping toward noon. Devi beams a message to Winnipeg asking for an estimated time of arrival of her next assignment, and what she gets back doesn't enthuse her. Perhaps as a result of the floods that have recently ground to a halt substantial chunks of the

Texas economy, her dispatcher – who signs off as Garth in a playful dig – says there are very few outbound loads to be had. And so we wait, and wait, and wait.

Devi decides we should pass the time in more inviting confines. She drives to the parking lot of a shopping mall, parks her rig away from the crowds, and – after she tethers Posh's leash to the side-view mirror – she goes shopping.

I am nominated to stand guard – or, in this case, sit guard. I type a few words on my laptop, wave out the window to Posh, and, although I don't solicit the conversation, speak to the mall security guard – a scrawny freckled fellow in big pants – who gets out of his car and tells me, "You're going to have to move this thing 'fore too long." I say, "The driver's in the mall, spending money." He mumbles something and heads off.

It's an hour later, and Devi returns. "Crappy mall," she says, checking the Qualcomm, finding no word. So we walk to a deli on the other side of the parking lot and get a sandwich. We walk to the coffee shop and sip a beverage. We return to the truck and sit there, paralyzed without purpose. Then finally, at half past three, there's a beep from the satellite and a message. But it's not the one Devi was hoping for. It says: "Head for Houston." It means there is nothing doing in Dallas. It means she is heading for Houston only to increase her odds of deployment. There is not yet a load for her to fetch. There may or may not be one tomorrow.

"This doesn't happen very often," she says, "but when it does, it stinks."

It stinks because now, as rush hour is reaching its height, she is making a two- or three-hour run with the express purpose of sleeping in the hotel room her company provides in the case of a no-load layover. It's a bad situation for both parties: the company is out the expense of the hotel plus twenty-five dollars a night layover pay, and the driver – who obviously cannot subsist on twenty-five dollars a night – isn't otherwise getting paid until the truck is loaded and rolling.

And so she sparks up the motor and begins the slow roll. She drives past Coffee City (population 193) and Dogwood City (population 800); past roadside slews filled deep enough to engulf a truck; past a Wal-Mart distribution centre in a city called Palestine, a roadside sea of tractors and trailers lining up to service the world's biggest retailer. She points out the latter with particular enthusiasm.

"The trucker's best friend is Wal-Mart," she says. "Because I would say the majority of Wal-Mart stores you can get a truck into. Huge parking lots. I was thinking of getting a Wal-Mart tattoo, but I think that would be a little extreme. Garth is enough."

Wal-Mart isn't considered the trucker's best friend in some quarters. While Devi enjoys the wide selection and unparalleled prices that the world's largest retailer provides, it is the way Wal-Mart conducts its business that, in a lot of ways, has quickened trucking's pace to breakneck. The Arkansas-based conglomerate is one of the industry leaders in just-in-time inventory strategy, a set of management practices first developed by the Toyota Motor

Company that has become a standard operating procedure for companies in many industries. In Toyota's native Japan, a country the size of Montana with a population of 127 million, acquiring scarce land for large warehouses is impractical and uneconomic. Initially thought to be a disadvantage, this lack of space led to innovation. Systems were redesigned to account for the lack of inventory on hand. On the automobile assembly line, for instance, there might be room for the storage of one particular part. That part's usage triggered a signal in the supply chain that another part was required.

Other companies were quick to see the advantages of the Japanese system. Now, decades later, the world's most competitive retailers have become the world's most efficient distributors of their goods. Wal-Mart, the world's largest company in terms of revenue in 2004, has been an industry groundbreaker on this front. It invested in a point-of-sale inventory system in the 1980s, a then-expensive but ultimately cost-efficient software suite that ensured that when a Gas Barbecue Model 1 was rung through the checkout in Buffalo, another Gas Barbecue Model 1 was readied for shipment to that location. It has ensured the quick delivery of products by building its stores within a day's drive of its distribution centres. It has also amassed one of the largest private trucking fleets in the United States, a 5,000-some-strong collection of tractors and 23,000 trailers that allow the company to control its transportation costs better than its competitors.

The just-in-time model couldn't work without North America's fast and reliable trucking companies.

On the road, I yawn. All the sitting is making me drowsy. I ask Devi how she manages to stay awake.

"It can take anything to wake you up; nearly driving in the ditch, nearly hitting the truck in front of you," she says. "I have power naps, I just don't lie down to have 'em. I always say to people, I do some of my best sleeping right behind the wheel. But after my little incident in 1990, I don't get to that point. I have a totally different driving style. Back then, I would do the expedited stuff, the illegal stuff, just go, go, go. Now I don't do it."

The little incident in 1990 ended with her truck overturned in the snow near Swift Current in the wee hours of a Saskatchewan morning, with Devi hanging upside down from her seat belt wondering what had happened. And it nearly ended worse: a man approaching the scene of her single-vehicle accident told her that because the road was unlit and because he happened to be dozing off, he nearly slammed into the belly of her truck.

"I don't ever want to die at the wheel of a truck," she says. "If I ever die behind a wheel of a truck, I want everyone to know that up there, I'm looking down and I'm mad as hell and I want to know why that happened. Was I an idiot out here? Did I do something to cause that? Did somebody else do something to cause my death? Was I at the wrong place at the wrong time? I don't ever want to die out here. And a lot of guys say they love trucking so much and happiness to them would be to drive off a cliff and die in a truck because they'd be doing something they love.

"But dying in a truck is a horrific death. You fall off the side of a mountain. You crash your truck and you burn to death. You crash your truck and you die slowly behind the wheel because nobody's coming to get you quickly enough. I think about it. It's terrible, especially when I see accidents and I see other people dying. And it's like, 'There by the grace of God go I.' It straightens out your driving for about two seconds. You drive a little more careful. But after my little wreck, my driving certainly has changed.

"Have I done some stupid things? Yeah, near misses. Reached down to pick something up and realized you're now three feet into that lane and there's a Cadillac you're pushing into the ditch. And you're like, 'Oh my God, I'm so embarrassed. Thank God nothing happened.' It's like the fish that got away story. 'Yeah, I almost wiped out a Cadillac. Thank God I didn't.' I could never live with myself if I caused an accident. Imagine killing somebody?"

Death, though, is a highway fixture. About eight people die in fatal traffic accidents in Canada every day; about eleven times more in the States. And though studies have repeatedly shown that when a car and a truck collide, it is the driver of the car who is far more often at fault (in as many as 80 per cent of cases), it is also the driver of the car who is far more likely to die. Trucks – by no fault of their drivers, by their sheer size and weight – kill people. And trucks, too, when they kill people repeatedly in any given media centre – especially over the span of a slow news period – have been known to cause a certain hysteria in the headlines and on the talk-radio airwaves. In 1996, when runaway truck wheels killed three motorists in a thirteen-month span in and around Toronto, there was an outcry like the Canadian trucking industry has rarely weathered. There were calls for the banning of trucks from urban highways, which would have left urbanity in short supply of supplies. There were calls to build trucks-only thoroughfares, calls to prosecute truckers who were negligent in servicing their vehicles with jail time worthy of a murderer. Even Devi's mother got on the phone.

"My mother is the only mother in history that called the trucking company her daughter worked for and asked if my lug nuts were tight," says Devi. "She did. All those wheels that were falling off on the 401? She calls up the owner of my company and says, 'People are dying, and all I want to know is, are my daughter's lug nuts tight?' But she was serious. She wanted to know what the service was like on our vehicles. Was the maintenance up to snuff?

"I said, 'Mom, you're the only mother that's ever called a trucking company and asked if the lug nuts were tight.' And she said, 'I don't care. I'm your mother.'"

Devi chose her truck, the Eagle 758, not for its tight lug nuts or its 420-horsepower CAT engine, but for the small glass window at the bottom of its passenger door. The window is designed to allow the driver to see if there's a vehicle directly beside the truck, traditionally one of a truck's handful of problem-inducing blind spots. But from the moment Devi took the truck for a test drive, Posh showed little interest in the window's merits as a safety feature. The dog adopted the piece of glass as her own, staring through it like a teenager might stare at a TV screen. She didn't seem to mind that the view was low-brow – that, because Devi spent most of her time in the far-right lane, the tiny window looked out mostly on rumble strips and weedy shoulders. Posh clouded the glass with a slow river of drool.

Devi spoils her pooch. When the truck-stop pavement simmers, in the south or in the summer, she fits Posh's paws with cushioned booties for the walk to the grassy lavatory. When the dog dish is empty, it is filled exclusively with bottled water, Aberfoyle Springs, which Devi buys by the case and stores in a compartment beneath her sleeper. When the ride is long and the cab is filled with whimpering, biscuits materialize to soothe the complaints.

As we roll toward Houston – our first extended period of transit and a period of adjustment for the dog, who isn't accustomed to the annoyance of a human who doesn't dote – Posh attempts to assume her usual position on the floor in front of the passenger seat. But the grey carpet is currently occupied by a pair of black suede sneakers, Converse size elevens. The dog nudges the intruder's ankle with her nose. She grunts her displeasure. And when the drool soaks through a sock, the offending sneakers lift like a palace gate and the resident princess stretches out luxuriously, pressing her snout against her beloved window on the world.

Says Devi: "Ahhh. Poshie needs room. Poshie needs her window."

All around us are trucks. There are refrigerated trailers, "reefers" in the parlance, that can typically be identified by the grilled protrusions bolted to the top of the front of the trailer, not to mention the considerable buzzing that accompanies the operation of these cooling systems. A couple of generations ago the truckers who hauled perishable goods from, say, Florida's citrus groves to the markets of Saskatoon, kept their cargo fresh by covering it in layers of ice. Their warm-weather northbound trail was marked by the constant drip of the melt. Their trips were interrupted by stops to replenish the ice's depth, not to mention to acquire a large block to place in the cab in lieu of air conditioning. Oldtimers swore by the ice's effectiveness in keeping the produce in A-grade shape and the ice block's surprising effects on its surrounding air temperature. Plus, ice was quieter. The wee-hours arrival of a humming reefer in a truck-stop parking lot makes few friends of truckers struggling to sleep.

There are chrome-tubed tankers. There are standard doubles, which consist of two trailers, each 28 feet long. There are turnpike doubles, which consist of two 53-foot or 48-foot trailers pulled in tandem, and there are Rocky Mountain doubles, a 53-foot or 48-foot trailer followed by another 28-feet long. However, there are no triples, three 28-footers in succession (known as road trains), a commonplace sight on Australia's loneliest roads, but still illegal in many states and provinces, despite lobbying from the industry. The Aussies know excess: in 1999, the folks at Guinness certified a book-worthy record for the world's longest road train, a forty-five-trailer juggernaut that measured the length of nearly six Canadian football fields and was pulled by a Kenworth tractor for some eight kilometres. The mark was toppled in 2003 when a tractor – or, in Australian, a prime mover – towed eighty-seven trailers stretching more than twice the length of the previous record holder. The problem with road trains, of course, is passing them. And that is part of the reason why the North American trucking industry's attempts to get longer trailers legalized have been staunchly opposed by critics, chiefly the railroad lobby. The naysayers point out that although the trailers in triples are permitted to be a standard thirteen feet high, their shorter wheelbase makes them less stable than their longer brethren. Advocates cite the benefits of permitting triples the run of the roads. The argument goes that truck trips would be reduced, as would wear and tear on roads; distributing weight over more axles, the physics suggest, makes for lighter treading on asphalt.

No matter the configuration, they're all known as semi-trailers – semi because they carry only a portion of their own weight. The trailers connect to the tractors at a horseshoe-shaped pivot point the size of a small manhole known as the fifth wheel. It's an inaccurate moniker, since most tractors are possessed of ten wheels – two on the front axle, and four on each of the two rear, or drive, axles grouped in side-by-side pairs known as doubles. Most trailers have eight wheels, two axles with two sets of doubles apiece. Thus: eighteen-wheeler.

Suddenly our faces are bathed in the glow of brake lights. Traffic is heavy and we are crawling toward Houston. Voices on the CB moan about the congestion, about the lack of loads in the surrounding vicinity. Devi says, "See. We're not the only ones." And through the drawls on Channel 19 comes a weary voice speaking in a more familiar tongue.

"The problem with the trucking business," says the voice, "is that everybody's trying to cut everybody else's throat. You can't make a decent buck any more."

The doomsayer is Raith, a twenty-eight-year-old Winnipegger who coincidentally drives for the same company as Devi – although they've never met face and face – and is similarly stuck in these faraway parts without a load. He is heading to the Flying J (a popular chain of truck stops) in East Houston to park and sleep and hope for a more lucrative tomorrow. Devi's destination is the same.

So before long we're sitting at a table at a truck stop ordering Cokes and coffees and waters while Raith – a tall and bony slip of a man with a shaved head and a scraggly beard – tells the story of how, a couple of years back, his Qualcomm was beeping at what he deemed ridiculous intervals. This was before he worked for Winnipeg Motor Express, he says, when his dispatcher seemed to take pleasure in harassing him needlessly (a common complaint of the trade). Raith, the story goes, picked up the noisy terminal and tossed it out the passenger window, laughing down the road as it flapped against the side of his tractor, its cord stretching to its limit, its beep mercifully imperceptible over the windblown racket.

"I finally pulled it back into the truck because I got tired of the noise," he says, sipping his Coke. "All these other truckers got on the radio and said, 'Wow! I wish I could do that.' And I said, 'If you want to do it, just do it.'"

Qualcomm's technology has changed the lives of truckers. Before its introduction in 1988 and until it became ubiquitous in the mid-1990s, many trucking companies used rudimentary filing systems to keep track of shipments and drivers. Satellite antennas that mounted on the roof of a truck's cab were previously uncommon because their cost, as much as two thousand dollars, wasn't feasible. It wasn't unusual for companies to store the crucial information on index cards. And it was all but impossible to reach a trucker until he called the dispatcher to report on his whereabouts. But Qualcomm's innovation included a relatively tiny satellite dish, less than a foot in diameter, that sold for about two hundred dollars. It was promptly adopted by most of the major trucking companies and even the U.S. government, which trusted it enough to keep tabs on shipments of ammunition and nuclear waste.

Raith laughs at his own story. Then, as if to keep the comedy bit going, he lifts his arms off the table, extending them like a zombie sleep-walking from the grave. His hands, his fingers, the muscles in his skinny forearms – they are all visibly shaking.

"I'm vibrating," he says. "I feel like I'm stoned. I haven't been out of the truck all day."

He hasn't been home in a few weeks, either, and he says that although his runs seem to get longer – although his job gets more and more taxing in time and frustration and lack of sleep – his bottom line sinks lower.

"Everything goes up but your paycheques," he says. "But the worst part about it is putting up with the traffic. Especially in the summertime – it's tourist season, but we're not allowed to shoot 'em."

This time he doesn't laugh at his own joke. He shakes his head and looks into his lap and says, "I've got to get out of this business . . ."

Devi calls for the bills and says we should be going. We bid Raith goodbye and climb into the truck to find our hotel, which presents itself quickly from the roadside, a shiny new Super 8 with a gleaming concrete parking lot that – at the size of a football field – suffices. We order pizza and watch the Country Music Awards. Garth Brooks, on a hiatus that has seen him spend more time taking batting practice with the New York Mets than writing the next hit Devi is anticipating, is sadly absent from the show's roster.

After a short night's sleep and yet another Texas-style continental breakfast – this time sugar doughnuts and Froot Loops – we're back in the parking lot of the East Houston Flying J in what seems like an instant. It's a perfect morning. There's a breeze and a speckless sky. But there is no joy via satellite, no message on the Qualcomm bidding Devi good morning. She parks her truck in one of the rare empty spots and soon she's on the phone to Willy, the dispatcher.

"Honey, what's doing?" she says. "How many of us are in Texas? And don't lie to me."

It turns out that Devi's company has far more drivers in Texas – and especially Houston – than it has loads to disperse. Business is so slow that one of the Houston loiterers has been dispatched to San Antonio, some six hundred miles north. "And that," says Devi, "is not a good sign . . . He says some of the drivers are starting to get cranky."

As we walk into the truck stop, Devi pauses to talk to a scruffy-looking man in a Green Bay Packers shirt who is, we learn, accompanied by a Shih Tzu named Coco. He introduces himself as John Coren, a retired meat inspector for Canada's federal government who, flush with a healthy pension, has taken to the road as a second career. He is standing next to his truck, the windshield of which is skirted by comic-strip dialogue bubbles etched with common-sense mantras such as "Trust in God but Lock Your Car."

"I'm empty now," he says, referring to his trailer. "I'm stranded."

John and his wife, Sandy, had been making the truck their home for the past few years, seeing the continent in their retirement dream, but Sandy died a couple of months back. "It hasn't been easy," he says, "but it's like a holiday for me. I'm using this job as a way of seeing all the states."

We all head inside to sit and wait. The place is busy – the lounge is full, the three pay phones are lined up (maybe because there are so few of them in this cellphone era), the arcade is loud with action. We run into Raith, who is playing video billiards, slapping a track ball with long-fingered fervour.

"Tension breaker," he says.

Devi and I sit down in the restaurant. John Coren joins us after a trip to the shower. He has doffed the cap he'd been wearing, a Confederate-soldier knock-off, and he has parted his thinning grey hair sternly to the side. He has also put in his dentures. I know this because he shows me with a clenched smile right after he says, "I feel like I lost ten pounds." He means in dirt, in the shower.

Soon Raith is rounding out the Canadian foursome.

"You need menus?" asks the waitress.

"Yes, ma'am," says Devi. "And a load."

"A load?" says the waitress. "Well, you're in the right place for a load. They'll tell you a load." She motions to the room, where, by my count, twenty-two drivers are slouched over nosh. Only two of them are not wearing trucker caps, those high-riding derivations of the baseball cap that, along with being part of the default uniform of choice for truckers unwilling to sport Stetsons, which one still sees occasionally in Southwest truck stops, became an accoutrement of choice for urban hipsters in the early part of the 2000s.

Flying J is named for founder Jay Call, a Utah Mormon with a passion for aviation and, according to the company's website, "a fetish for cleanliness," who started a company that has become North America's largest marketer of diesel fuel, the thirty-fifth largest private company in the United

States in 2004 according to *Forbes* magazine. Call died
when the plane he was piloting crashed five miles south of
Sun Valley, Idaho, in 2003, but his chain of travel plazas,
168 at last count in forty-one states and three provinces,
with thirty more stops under construction, lives on healthily. They bill what are commonly known as truck stops as
travel plazas these days, because there's always a set of
regular gasoline pumps on the other side of the building
from the truck-sized diesel pumps. It's not just truckers
stopping here. It's recreational-vehicle enthusiasts and
vacationing motorists and territory-covering salespeople
and local folks.

But for truckers the travel plazas are like ports of call,
the hubs of a life spent on the periphery of life, on the outskirts of cities, at the junction of highways. And so the
stores therein often provide a vast array of products for
the transient clientele. At the Flying J's outlet on the edge
of London, Ontario, for instance, one can buy Can-O-Scent
air freshener in jasmine and cherry flavours, a professional
poker set in a lightweight reinforced aluminum case, a
CB antenna, a tub of premium citrus pumice hand cleaner,
a fourteen-inch television-VCR combo, a power inverter, a
refrigerator-air-purifier that claims to kill "96 per cent of
bacteria, mold and fungi," a DC electric shaver that plugs
into a cigarette lighter, a sign that says "Wide Load" or
"Oversized Load," flare kits, padlocks, manicure sets, cat
food, blue jeans, toy trucks in 1:32 scale die-cast metal with
doors that open, licorice allsorts, a thirty-minute videotape
labelled "Snowboard Mayhem," a T-shirt with a front that

reads "What's the definition of a Canadian?" and a back that reads "An unarmed American with healthcare," a CD audio book of *George Foreman's Guide to Life* read by George Foreman, a sixteen-CD set of *James Earl Jones Reads the Bible*, squeegees, a six-inch electric frying pan that plugs into a cigarette lighter, and a pocket guide to North American truck stops that lists five thousand "park-able truck stops."

There is considerable competition in the truck-stop business, although the move away from independently owned operations toward corporate monoliths continues. As recently as a decade ago, some 60 per cent of the member truck stops of the U.S. National Association of Truck Stop Operators were independents. Now more than 60 per cent of member stops are links in a chain. Pilot Travel Centers owns more locations than Flying J; the Tennessee-based conglomerate has made it a practice to buy out competitors and, to the chagrin of many owner-operators, raise pump prices. But Pilot's pump price, which is often a few cents higher than the list price at surrounding truck stops, is deceiving. Most of its clients, company drivers for large carriers, pay far lower pre-negotiated prices for their diesel. It's the owner-operators who don't have the buying power of a large fleet who are left to pay the advertised price.

These other men in Devi's life – the thousands of fellow truckers with whom she shares the road, the airwaves, and the limited parking spaces – have mostly been kind to her. She dines with them and talks with them. She has even, she says, gone to movies with men whose names she did not know. But there have been nasty exceptions. She once made the mistake of cutting off a driver who, in pursuit of revenge – and unbeknownst to Devi – followed her into a truck stop many miles down the road and tapped on her door. When she swung the door open, unaware she'd been tailed, she was greeted by a scowl wearing brass knuckles. She said, "J.B. Hunt, right?" He said, "Yes." She said, "By the way, I did not cut you off on purpose. I accidentally cut you off." And he said, "Well, I thought you were a typical driver being an asshole to a J.B. Hunt truck and that you did it on purpose." He said, "I can assure you these were going to be in your face, but I can't do that now."

Says Devi: "And I was fine. But had I been a guy, I would have probably been dead or close to it."

It's coffee and waters all around at the table. Talk, as it always seems to, turns to prostitution. Raith says he has never partaken, though he was recently tempted.

"One of them was kind of cute," he says. "I was thinking about how much money I have left."

"Well, I don't think you need much," says Devi.

"I still haven't done that, yet," says Raith.

"Don't say yet," she says.

"They come out like cockroaches. It's hard to keep beating them back."

Coren laughs: "Laredo's bad. They've even got a guy dressed up as a girl. That was fun. I knew a driver named Adrien picked him – or her? – up. We waited for about fifteen minutes and all hell broke loose in that truck."

Everybody laughs, but this is no relaxing sit-down. There's an antsy edge to these conversations. They're all waiting impatiently for work. They're not making real money sitting in this booth. And if they're not making real money, they'd rather be elsewhere.

Finally, for Devi – who's been checking in with dispatch every hour on the hour – there is word of work. It's a load with her name on it on the other side of town. She writes down the details and makes the call, arranging the pickup with the shipper.

It means another night at the Super 8. But it's an early wake-up call and we arrive at the customer's docks at 7:20 a.m., even though the place doesn't open for business until 8:00, and there's already another truck idling in wait, its cab curtains drawn tight. This, Devi says, is when she usually cleans her house, when she pulls out a container of baby wipes and dusts her vast dashboard, when she plugs in her vacuum – it's a Dirt Devil – and goes to work. But in this case, because she's been without a purpose for the past forty-eight hours or so, there isn't much to be done.

Houston's industrial end is almost beautiful at this hour, neat rows of warehouses strung on a white concrete grid. The low sun casts flattering light on the sprawling blight. I squint to the east and see a black man in a soiled green jacket approach the truck, a stained blue hood obscuring his eyes. He offers to sweep out Devi's trailer. He asks for five dollars. She declines.

"Five dollars – is he serious?" she says. "That's eight bucks Canadian. That's parking-lot robbery."

At the stroke of eight, Devi hops to the tarmac and approaches the warehouse door. She walks in to the drone of production and the hum of fluorescence and stands in front of the window to an office. But there is nobody in the office. Workers are buzzing by – bidding each other good morning, slapping each other on the shoulder of their standard-issue blue work shirts – but there is no actual sign of work being done. It's 8:15 when I count nine employees standing around talking and laughing outside a loading dock. Devi has been joined by a red-headed grandmother who hauls refrigerated cargo out of North Carolina and who is telling stories about having her truck ransacked in New York City. The employees look at the truckers standing a few feet away, but they don't acknowledge the women.

"These people are getting paid," says Devi. "And we're sitting here not getting paid."

Finally, at 8:20, there is stirring in the office. A woman with a grey cardigan pulled over her shoulders slides open the window to service her visitors, and the red-headed stranger, without a word, springs toward the door and jumps the queue of two.

"She's nothing more than a bully," whispers Devi, rolling her eyes. "I'm not going to stand here and have a fight with her."

Things improve quickly, though. In minutes Devi's paperwork has been handed off to James, the plant's shipper, who is smoking a plastic-tipped cigar and furiously flipping through mounds of crinkled invoices.

He says to Devi, "I need you at Door 14."

Devi says, "Is this one of those processes that's going to take all day?"

James says, "You'll probably be here one hour and you'll be on the road."

Devi: "Well, that's acceptable."

"That's acceptable? That's good. Most places you'd be here all day."

"Yeah, you're right."

James is true to his estimate: in sixty-five minutes the trailer is loaded with twenty-two pallets – 38,796 pounds – of plastic resin tablets, a raw material used in the production of plastics.

James twirls his cigar in his fingers as he bids his customer adieu: "So y'all will be in Canada by tomorrow night?"

"We would be if it was legal, but it's not," says Devi.

James laughs.

"What kind of a truck driver is legal?"

Devi smiles a knowing smile and leads the way off the loading dock and back into the truck. She pulls away from the loading dock with a quick jolt, then hops out of the truck to swing shut her door, telling the story as she does of the time she drove to Saskatoon in a snowstorm and arrived to find her once-empty trailer filled with snow because she forgot to close the trailer doors.

Our departure is moments away. But before we head out Devi has two orders of business. First, she pulls her truck onto the scale to ensure she's within legal limits, which she is. Then, she removes her shoes and slides into slippers, unbuckles her belt, unbuttons her faded Levis, and unzips them, too.

"You'll have to forgive me," she says. "I drive with my pants open. It's just uncomfortable to have tight jeans around your gut, so I'm forever saying, 'Hang on, I've got to get my pants on' before I leave the truck."

She also downs two tablets of Pepto-Bismol and opens her window to make a slight adjustment to her side-view mirror. And by 10:00, with a big Houston sun transforming a cool morning into a toasty noon, we're driving north.

There isn't much scenery on this Texas expressway bordered by scrub and full ditches. But there are billboards. We're passing advertisements for "Boiled P-Nuts" and "E-Z Bail Bonds" and "Double Wides $199/month."

"The American Dream," says Devi. "Thank God I'm Canadian."

We're passing, too, a white shack boarded up and tilting on its foundation: "Going Out of Business." Traffic is light. Devi is sustaining a respectable speed for the first time since I joined her, keeping the needle at about sixty-six miles per hour. I start to notice, a couple of hours into our journey, that her truck – although it's filled with amenities – isn't exactly outfitted with a Cadillac's boat-smooth suspension.

"How would you like to bounce around like this all day long?" she asks.

The truth is, I'm not liking it much. The passenger seat has sub-economy legroom. It borders on torturous. With every bump in the road, my knees are thrust dangerously close to my chest, and because Posh is occupying the floor in front of me, my options for repositioning my feet, for stretching my legs, are nil.

Devi asks me repeatedly if I'm comfortable, and I say I am. But there's numbness in my hamstrings and an increasing ache in my back. Before long I'm thinking about the words of the doctor who once treated my faulty lumbar with a prescription of muscle relaxants that put me to sleep not long after he offered this word of advice: "You should avoid long drives."

Devi most definitely looks comfortable. There's a beguiling confidence in the way she conducts the business of barrelling north, as though every highway is her own. She acknowledges, though, that her trusty machine is a rough rider. That's not to say it's as uncomfortable as the trucks twenty years its senior; many of those were outfitted with what drivers came to term hockey-puck suspensions, with all the cushion of frozen rubber. These days, though, the finest long-haul cruisers achieve luxurious rides reminiscent of European-engineered sedans. Devi's being a company-owned truck, it's bereft of the frills that you'd find on such top-line iron.

"I need to get custom brassieres made just to drive this truck," she laughs. "Everything is sore between my belly button and my Adam's apple. The first time I took this truck out of the yard, I came back a week later and I said, 'Okay, who's going to pay for the new bras?'"

We pull into Love's Truck Stop at Rd. 841 for lunch; we're just outside of Nacogdoches, which bills itself as the

"oldest town in Texas." Devi faxes some paperwork ahead
to Canada Customs. We order submarine sandwiches and
take a seat.

I'm looking at the map, planning an exit. Because of
the long wait in Houston, I'm going to have to fly home
from another port before the Canadian border. I make a
phone call checking on flights out of Memphis, which is
another seven hours up the road. Devi, too, is thinking
about home.

"I own my own condo in Winnipeg, and when you
walk in, you'll just die," she says. "It's like a museum in
there. I mean, it's very fancy, in the respect that I've got
lots of art. Everything's neat and clean. It's high class and
expensive, you know? It's how I was raised so I just contin-
ued that kind of a life. You walk in and you would never in
a million years say, 'There's a truck driver that lives here.'"

She has a roommate named Brad, a golf pro who brings
to the household $380 in monthly rent, a fifty-one-inch-
screen TV, and an aversion to close contact with cleaning
products.

"I have been in truck stops in the middle of nowhere
and this bathroom" – the one Devi and Brad share – "isn't
as clean."

It's a good thing, then, that she uses truck-stop bath-
rooms far more than she uses the one at the Terraces of
Tuxedo, where she sleeps in her condo maybe sixty nights
a year.

"Drivers always say they have diesel fuel running
through their veins and it totally controls you and runs you.

And as soon as you start running low on diesel and you start sputtering out, it's time for another trip," she says. "It's like a drug almost. They say they hate it, but as soon as they get out of the business, most of them, they don't know what to do with themselves. They get claustrophobic in their own city and their own town, and that's the way I am now."

She says she has considered leaving this life, trying her hand at advertising maybe, or marketing, or promotions. The Dream Chaser Rally wouldn't be a bad centrepiece of a resume. "My dad always says, 'You're a truck driver but you have so many ideas. You're wasting your talent.'"

The thing is, she says, she has tried living in one city before. Even in Winnipeg – even in the middle of the vast flatland, where many of the residents speak of the liberating luxury of seemingly boundless space – she feels hemmed in.

"In my head I know there's a perimeter [road] around the city, and when I'm in Winnipeg, I feel completely confined by that perimeter," she says. "It's like, whether I'm home for twenty-four hours or very rarely I'm home for a few days, it's like, 'Time to leave.'

"I have to be able to leave. I've been leaving this city since I was twenty years old, just driving out and having the freedom of just going."

We leave the truck stop, and we're back on the trail, zipping through a Bible Belt afternoon one mile per hour over the sixty-five-mph speed limit. The Interstate is almost empty. The scenery is unremarkable. Devi turns on the CB for a while, but the chatter is as scattered as the traffic.

The airwaves are often far livelier. The citizens' band radio was introduced in the United States in the 1940s, but it didn't become especially popular until the late 1960s, when the technology became affordable for the average trucker. By the 1970s, truckers couldn't afford not to have one; they became especially vital as a means of warning other drivers about police speed traps when the U.S. government, in response to a spike in oil prices and fear of an energy shortage, lowered the national speed limit to fifty-five miles per hour in 1974.

But the CB got bigger than your average workplace tool. It was romanticized in popular culture, perhaps most pervasively in "Convoy," a hit song by C.W. McCall that interspersed an age-of-Aquarius chorus with the fictional radio dispatches of a long line of truckers thundering through the American night with regard for neither trooper nor speedometer. The single sold some 5 million copies between 1975 and 1976, around the same time that the U.S. Federal Communications Commission saw applications for CB licences go from a trickle (73,375 in January 1975) to a certifiable fad (more than 500,000 in January 1976). Betty Ford, the president's wife, was said to have a CB and a handle, "First Mama." Muhammad Ali, the heavyweight boxing champion, was a natural ratchet jaw, his ears occasionally on. Even Snoopy got in on the action from his doghouse in the *Peanuts* comic strip. Everyone knew that 10-4 means "heard you loud and clear." Fewer folks, enthusiasts mostly, knew that 10-5 means "I'll relay the message"; that 10-6 means "I'm busy. Hang on"; that 10-11 means "You're talking too fast"; that 10-55 was code for an intoxicated driver; and 10-73 was code for speed trap.

But CB chatter isn't so much a number-heavy code as it is a living language with a not-so obvious vocabulary. You need to know a bear isn't a grizzly, but a highway patrolman. A bear in the air is a police aircraft. A bear bite is a speeding ticket. A gator isn't a reptile; it's the carcass of a done tire. A dog is a Greyhound bus.

You need to know Chicago is the Windy, Nashville the Guitar, Miami the Bikini. The Rubber is Akron, Ohio, home of the Goodyear Tire Company. You need to know a bedbugger is a moving truck; a parking lot is an automobile carrier. A meat wagon isn't a cattle truck; it's an ambulance. A chicken hauler is a chicken hauler. A bumper sticker isn't a bumper sticker; it's a four-wheeler following too closely. A deadhead isn't a follower of the psychedelic jam band, it's a trip on which a trucker travels with an empty trailer. A reefer doesn't get you high; it gets your produce to the market in refrigerated comfort. Your travel agent doesn't book Caribbean getaways; he's your dispatcher. A skateboarder doesn't do tricks on ramps; he's a driver of a flatbed truck. You need to know the passing lane is the hammer lane and the slow one's the granny. That a salt shaker plows snow. And you need to know how to converse. Calling somebody "Good buddy" is not good etiquette. Addressing your colleagues as "Driver" will do fine. If you're speaking to a particular driver, refer to him by his truck's make – as in, "Yo, Freightliner" – or by his company's name. To say, "J.B. Hunt, you got it on?" is to ask the driver's-seat occupant if he's listening to Channel 19. To say, "Breaker-breaker" is to expose oneself as a poseur.

Sober watchdogs of the public good were taken aback at the CB's 1970s popularity. *Time* magazine worried that the CB had "not only nourished a proliferating vocabulary that threatens to outdate any dictionary of American slang within months" but that the new medium "catalyzes an egalitarian, anti-authoritarian philosophy that has never been expressed in this fashion before." The *New York Times* was more upbeat: "If the people who use [CB] and the people who regulate its use can prevent it from becoming a monster, it might well have a cultural and social impact on American life almost as profound as the last electronic communications gadget to sweep the country – the television set."

It had no such impact, of course, except on the lives of truckers, who still rely on its virtues for everything from speed-trap callouts to traffic tips to the solicitation of prostitution. The proliferation of small-minded blather has led some veterans of the trade to dub it the Children's Band, but there remain forty channels to choose from. Channel 9 is reserved for emergency use. Channel 19 is the unofficial truckers' channel. It's not uncommon for drivers who strike up a conversation on 19 to switch to another channel for more privacy, although there is no such thing. It's not unlike an Internet chat room; there is the lack of accountability that goes with anonymity. A popular 1970s song, "CB Savage" by Rod Hart, tells the tale of an effeminate-sounding trucker whose double-entendre-rife transmissions distract the good-old-boy truckers in the vicinity. In the track's punchline, the voice morphs into a stern state trooper's drawl, and the convoy of truckers who've been taken aback by the presence on the airwaves of an honest-to-goodness homosexual get nabbed for speeding.

The march of technology has changed the medium. Two truckers who really want to talk will exchange cell-phone numbers and tune out the chatter, which has become infinitely less listenable since the advent of power boosters that allow tech-savvy enthusiasts to transmit signals that are far louder than the average 10-4. Nobody says 10-4 any more. Nobody says breaker-breaker. But hobbyists bent on drawing attention to themselves can begin to approximate the sound of God speaking to Moses on the Mount, the product of new-fangled effects units that soak the voices of lonely men in echo-chamber effects.

The average range of communication is one to five miles, but even low-powered transmitters can be heard for thousands of miles depending on the state of sun-spot activity. The signals bounce – or skip, in the lingo – off the ionosphere, causing interference that degrades the quality of communications, which is what we are hearing now, as Devi steers us past a sign – "In Trouble? Pray" – not far from a decrepit house whose roof has been patched with garbage bags and what looks like silver duct tape. We are hearing static, white noise on the CB radio.

"You get a lot of holy roller truck drivers down here. I shouldn't really call them that, but they're very religious, and they try to push their religion on you. They put these

stickers on their trucks, 'Property of God.' And I'm thinking, 'God's not making the payments on your truck, is he?'"

Devi laughs and tells of the time she met a Baptist
husband-wife team whose friendliness soon turned to
flat-out evangelism. The couple spent considerable time
and effort trying to make a convert out of their Canadian
acquaintance.

"The worst part was," says Devi, "they know I'm Jewish."

She is as Jewish, she says, "as a ham sandwich," not born
a child of Israel but adopted as one. Her first name isn't
her first name. She came into the world as a Tara-Lynn.
Her birth mother was seventeen.

"She shouldn't have named me," Devi says. "I ain't no
Tara-Lynn."

Devi, which means princess in Hindi, was bestowed by
the only parents she has ever known. They live in Toronto
now, as does her younger sister, who's a lawyer. Her brother,
an executive, lives in Los Angeles.

"I feel I'm extremely successful, as successful as my
sister," she says. "We're just in two completely different
types of work, but we're both very good and very successful, I think. There's a stigma attached to being a truck
driver. They bring it on themselves, the industry and the
drivers. I wish the drivers cared more and wanted to
elevate themselves and the industry. But they're perfectly
happy to just be the way they are. The schleps are happy
being the schleps."

Just then a gold truck approaches. It is crossing the

double yellow line and heading our way, and for a moment, I feel my body tighten. Then it veers back into its own lane, and Devi – who hadn't betrayed an ounce of consternation – laughs.

Prompted to recall her history of collisions, she rolls out a list: The family of deer she hit in Marquette, Michigan, a few years back (five animals abreast and every one involved in the melee), the deer that ran into the side of her truck, the owl that met her windshield in full flight.

Oh, and then there was that poor car in Calgary, over which she accidentally drove while carrying a load of Old Dutch potato chips. As a motorist, I failed to realize until Devi told me this story that stopping in front of a big rig's bumper – even at a seemingly harmless traffic light – can be a dangerous proposition. The long-nose design of many rigs, after all, doesn't allow their drivers to see what's immediately in front of them. To wit, Devi once crushed that Calgary sedan.

"Ah, stories you can tell the grandkids," she says.

Then she reaches back to pet Posh, who has offered my knees a brief respite by retreating to another favourite snoozing spot behind the seats. "I'll tell my grandpuppies, I guess."

She keeps driving, still mostly alone as we pass through Atlanta, Texas, past Dave Beard's Catfish King and Ed's Discount Store. It's a little after two o'clock, and after a long silence, there is suddenly lewd chatter coming from the CB. Devi turns down the sound and shakes her head. I ask her why she's kept her thumb off her CB-microphone trigger. She is, she says, not in the mood to be pursued. Her presence on the airwaves is rarely met with indifference.

The CB surfers usually start by asking if she has a husband. A boyfriend? And is she riding in a team with either of them. When she tells them, as she does, that she's a lone-riding woman, they suggest a conversation on a different channel, which is the CB equivalent of obtaining a phone number at a singles bar.

"Then they sweet-talk you. I'm nice to them. We go have lunch. They see I'm clean. I brush my teeth. And they want to marry you at the end of the day. Sometimes I feel like I'm leading them on. We're just objects for them to fantasize over. You open the door for them, and they walk in and sit down. Everybody's lonely out here. Everybody."

We drive and drive through a corridor of forest, and she talks of her habit of writing verse behind the wheel, her "sixty-five-mile-an-hour poems," and of her pen pal in England, who is fascinated by North American trucking because English lorries generally lack the chromium-plated sex appeal of their overseas superiors. The afternoon is slipping away. We hit the Arkansas state line around 4 p.m., roll through Hope, home of Bill Clinton, not long after. And soon we're in West Memphis, Ark., where she'll spend the night at a truck stop, and I'll catch a cab to the airport. In the bluish light of the hotel's parking lot, there is still more to say, and we walk and talk in the autumn chill, a day behind us, neither of our journeys near their end.

"I don't want to ever die, because I might miss something," she says. "You can't live forever and who wants to? I do. I've got things to accomplish, places to go, friends to meet. But I wouldn't wish this job on my worst enemy. To love it so much but to not wish it on anybody, it's hard to explain. It's like an oxymoron, I guess."

3

The Diamond Drive

I n the Edmonton airport, I watch a march to war a world away. Images of familiar adversaries flash on the departure-lounge screens; Saddam Hussein, the Iraqi dictator, vows to fight; George W. Bush, the U.S. president, promises victory. And as I flip through the morning papers, I feel a certain comfort to be flying to a place that has rarely been fought over.

In a Boeing 737-200 with a cargo hold far bigger than its passenger cabin – in a plane with room for just twenty-four passengers – the engines moan and we set off south, swinging quickly north, rising over the city's sprawling suburbs, over the North Saskatchewan River, half covered in white crust, half open-water blue. The landscape turns sparse quickly, the flats breaking up into perfect squares of farmland, the charcoal-coloured roads dividing the fields. It is a two-hour flight, and I doze until the rumble of our Yellowknife descent. We dip toward Great Slave Lake, a yawning abyss, its waves frozen ripples. And on the lake's vast surface – as the landing gear engages and my view improves – a complex topography is revealed: veins of mounding snow, black chasms of water, and blanched bumps and ridges. It is a warm day, minus-two Celsius, and there is a thick fog rising where water meets permafrost.

I have come here to ride along over a few hundred of the north's thousands of miles of ice roads, the network of white highways that, for a couple of months every year – from Nunavut to Alaska, from the northern extremes of Manitoba all the way west to British Columbia – transform the lakes and rivers of the coldlands into corridors of commerce. I arrive in Yellowknife as a hint of spring teases the locals with sunny warm days that give the ice that covers the city streets and sidewalks a teary sheen.

By the time I check into my hotel, as the sun rises above the horizon for its eight hours of face time, the temperature is well above freezing, six Celsius, and the massive goose-down parka I've brought along – complete with coyote-fur trim on the hood – is being made to look excessive by the locals, who happily go about their business with thin windbreakers unzipped, toques and gloves stuffed in pockets.

The warm spell doesn't only make me feel self-conscious. It threatens my plans. On the day I arrive, the overseers of the ice road I'd hoped to travel – a white highway that services Canada's pair of diamond mines – have decreed that daytime travel is prohibited. The sun is powerful enough to begin softening the road's surface, especially where it crosses the rocky stretches of cleared land that is flooded and re-flooded like a giant backyard shinny rink to connect the frozen bodies of water. The trucks – many of which weigh in at more than 120,000 pounds – could do irreparable damage to the so-called portages under such conditions.

"It's gotten so warm," says Janet Robinson, whose family has run an ice-road trucking operation out of Yellowknife for more than thirty years. "This is very unusual."

She makes good, though, on her promise to put me in a truck. I drive to the city's outskirts, to the compound where her family's business, Robinson Enterprises, makes its headquarters. There I am introduced to my travelling companion for an evening I'll long remember.

Alden Paul drops the cap of his Thermos on the gritty black floor of the truck drivers' kitchen, picks it up, and screws his coffee shut. There are other truckers huddled at picnic tables in the small room, men wearing a-few-days-old stubble atop the collars of quilted flannel jackets. There is the blue haze of unfiltered cigarettes, the smell of something burning. And there is a change in the air, too. This is the season's first foray into nights-only trucking, which means twenty-four hours' worth of traffic is going to be squeezed into the twelve hours between dusk and dawn.

"It's going to be back-to-back tonight," says Alden, who is speaking to a couple of his colleagues. "I pity the poor sonofabitch that spins out."

Alden leads me outside to the rear of the kitchen, and the scene, the sound is startling. An orchestra of idling diesels is parked in semi-circular lines. There are drivers inside the growling machines, men catching rest before a long journey. Alden has just awoken from his early-evening nap.

He asks me why I've come on this particular day. I say, "I guess I've got bad timing."

"No, you came at a good time," he says. "What you're going to see tonight only happens once a year. They talk about safety, half-a-mile apart, worrying about the ice, the waves. And tonight? Aw, fuck. They spend one night breaking all the rules they've built up."

The rules, I'll find out later, are fluid, although the laws of nature are absolute. Before the journey, we need fuel. We pull out of the lot and head for a nearby filling station. When we arrive, we find no attendant, no convenience store, just a computerized payment terminal in a phone-booth-sized shelter, where Alden inserts the relevant payment card and types in his PIN. I instinctively avert my eyes as he enters his code. He laughs: "You're used to being around bank machines. That number don't mean shit."

A moment earlier, he was informing me of the merits of the hand-held global positioning system he recently purchased. Suddenly the tank he was filling – one of the truck's two two-hundred-litre reservoirs – overflowed with diesel, splattering his blue jeans and soaking his parka's sleeve.

"Puawww!" he says. "Never done that before."

He ambles back to the truck, a white Western Star circa 1999. Western Star trucks were once built in Kelowna, British Columbia. But in 2000 the company was purchased by Freightliner, a pioneering trucking company that has been a subsidiary of a parent company – first Mercedes-Benz, then DaimlerChrysler – since 1981. And since 2002, Western Star trucks, which had long been engineered from headquarters in Cleveland, Ohio, have been produced in Portland, Oregon. Only the sleeper box, the part of the cab where the bunk is located, which, incidentally, is said to be far lighter than other sleeper boxes in the industry thanks to a honeycomb design, is made in Canada. Progress halts for no one. (Diamonds can no longer lay claim to being the hardest substance on the planet any more; that honour was ceded to aggregated diamond nanorods, an exotic form of carbon discovered by German physicists in 2005.) Only six months before, Alden and his son Colin sold most of their farm machinery and abandoned three generations of working the land on their plot in Smeaton, Saskatchewan. The father is matter of fact about his exit from agriculture. It's been a growing trend for a couple of decades, he says; a family operation, no matter how advanced, can't compete with the multinational super-farmers. So the independent farmer becomes the independent trucker, and, as Alden laughs, "The farmer turned trucker is still broke."

"It's about money, and farming was going soft," he says. "I'm not bad with the money, I can run the money pretty decent, but there was no income. We started getting a debt load that was not manageable. So we sold our iron, paid our bills off. We had enough left over to buy the truck Colin drives – well, not buy it outright but get a good down payment on it. We already had one, and then we traded the one we had for this one. Now we've got a '96 Star and a '99 Star."

He slams a door that bears the logo of the Saskatchewan Roughriders football team above the words, "Northwind Trucking Smeaton, Sask." He is wearing brown topsiders, a thin green parka, and faded blue jeans. His greying hair is buzzed tight, and he generally looks like a suburban soccer dad ready to watch a match on an autumn evening. His only visible nod to trucker fashion is a black leather ball cap that looks as though it has been slept in.

On the floor of Alden's cab is an assortment of white plastic bottles containing a variety of nutritional supplements, the likes of which I have never seen in or around a truck. There is a bottle containing cayenne pepper in capsule form. "It keeps me warm," Alden says. There are bottles marked Blue-Green Algae, Dandelion, Spirilina, and Vitamin C.

As we roll back to the Robinson yard, Alden informs me of this trip's purpose. In the stainless-steel bladders of his double-tanker trailers there are 47,500 litres of P40, a fuel used in small airplanes. His massive rig, a thirty-wheeler on eight axles, weighs about 62,500 kilograms. In moments we will be rejoining the idling congregation.

Drivers idle their trucks for a lot of reasons. In the Subarctic, it's conventional wisdom to keep the engine running at all times. During short stops, shutting off the engine dissipates the pressure that's built up in the air-brake system. It takes a few minutes for that pressure to return. They idle, too, because keeping the windows rolled down isn't much of an option. It's a security risk, for one. And it lets in fumes from a parking lot full of idling trucks. And there are a lot of days and nights when heat or air conditioning are required to get a decent sleep in the back berth. Some studies suggest that, in the United States, a typical trucker idles his engine between six and eight hours a day, some three hundred days a year.

The environmental and economic tolls are considerable. An idling truck consumes roughly four litres, or a U.S. gallon, of fuel an idling hour. That translates to about 1.2 billion gallons a year. (In 2005, when diesel prices topped out at more than US$3 per gallon in the wake of hurricanes Katrina and Rita, which shut down production at Gulf Coast oil refineries, that translated to about $4 billion spent going exactly nowhere.) It's expensive in other ways. Engines wear out quicker.

Diesel exhaust is no friend of the earth. It's filled with nitrogen oxides and sulfur dioxides, which contribute to the formation of acid rain; particulate matter, which can become lodged in the lungs and cause any number of health problems; carbon monoxide; hydrocarbons; and sulfur dioxide.

There are alternatives that haven't been widely embraced. There are small diesel-powered engines that can be retrofitted on cabs and provide electric power, air conditioning, and heat to both the driver's compartment and the engine and fuel lines. There are electric-powered units that install beneath the sleeper bunk and provide both heat and a/c.

Some 11 million tons of carbon dioxide are spewed into the atmosphere as a result, as are 180,000 tons of nitrogen oxides and 5,000 tons of particulate matter. But drivers have traditionally shirked alternatives to leaving their engines running. They sleep with their windows closed, no matter the weather, so even in the most comfortable times of the year they run the air conditioning or the heater or the fan. Gone are the days when hearty truckers enjoyed a night in the fresh air by snuggling in sleeping bags beneath their trucks. With all the idling going on outside at truck stops, truckers don't want to let the outside in.

"The outside" is how Alden and the other ice-road drivers refer to the rest of the world. Yellowknife has long been the centre of boom-and-bust mining eras, and in the early 1900s, when there were gold mines bustling north of the settlement, it was an isolated place. Supplies were expensive and scarce because the Subarctic weather made getting things to town nearly impossible. Much of the inventory in the local stores arrived by water over Great Slave Lake during the short summer. The spring's first barge was cause for an annual celebration. Yellowknife isn't exactly alone in the wilderness any more. The diamond mines north of the city – two actively producing jewels, another slated to open in the near future – have for a few years bestowed on the city a steady flow of new residents and new money.

I mention the state of the boom to Alden, but he claims to know little of the city's fortunes. Ice-road truckers reside in a job-induced netherzone. They are here to work, and they work until they go home. Only the need for sleep interrupts, or maybe the need for a night in a bar. Newspapers and magazines don't litter the barracks. There is no sitting-around time. And if there is a moment's rest, Alden says, "Your eyes should be closed.

"We know absolutely nothing about the war. We're in a cocoon up here."

As he speaks he is simultaneously driving and misting himself with the contents of a spray bottle. I recognize the smell of Windex. I say, "Are you spraying yourself with Windex?"

He continues to douse his shirt and his jeans, both victims of his fuel-pump accident: "Yeah, the ammonia kills the diesel smell."

I say, "Then what do you do about the ammonia smell?"

But Alden either isn't listening or doesn't hear me. He is busy turning the wheel into the Robinson yard, where his convoy is convening. The evening's trip will go like so: Colin will lead the four-truck group. Alden's friend Gary, a former RCMP officer, will follow Colin's trail with Alden behind him, and a man named Mike will bring up the rear.

In the street-light haze of the pot-holed parking lot, okays are exchanged on the CB, and the crawl begins. The foursome leaves the yard and proceeds to the check-in trailer of Nuna Logistics, the company that oversees the road and regulates its traffic. They park their trucks and make the short walk into the trailer. Inside, in the harsh light of a small space blinking with fluorescence, they slump around a small table and chat as they wait for the dispatcher to give them the all-clear.

Alden and Colin are talking tires.

"It's a misconception that we use special snow tires on the ice road," notes the son. "Traction isn't an issue. We use the same tires as your average highway rig."

They have a seventeen-hour journey ahead of them, and their eyes already appear weary. I am reading a notice on a bulletin board that details the ice road's strict speed limits. Loaded trucks aren't to travel faster than twenty-five kilometres an hour south of the Lockhart camp, an oasis for food and rest a little more than halfway to the mines. North of the Lockhart camp, where the ice is thicker, drivers can depress the accelerator until the needle hits thirty kilometres an hour.

The snail's-pace limits are a matter of survival. When a heavy truck drives over an ice-covered lake, the truck's force displaces water beneath the crust, creating a wave. At slow speeds, the wave is undetectable on the surface. But when the truck's velocity increases so, too, does the force of the sub-crust turbulence. Driving too fast – as the pioneering denizens of the ice roads found out – can make for a quick demise. A powerful enough wave, after all, will eventually find its way to the shoreline. Once at the junction of land and ice that wave will inevitably seek the path of least resistance – that is, through the ice – and blow a hole in the surface.

Lighter vehicles – say, the pickup trucks known as hotshots that transport personnel or urgent supplies to the mines – needn't heed the speed restrictions. Empty tractor-trailers, as a function of their reduced weight, also get a break. But for the vast majority of traffic, the pace can be maddeningly slow. What's worse is that on nights like this one, when heavy traffic is expected, speeds get slower still. When two trucks travelling in opposite directions pass each other on a lake, the chaotic turbulence of waves colliding has been known to cause chasm-exposing breaches in the ice. So for a northbound truck, the sight of a southbound requires a ten-kilometre-an-hour decrease in speed.

The possibility of such an ice-cracking disaster – and the lore of the unlucky truckers who have felt the chill of the Subarctic waters – is never far from the mind of the cautious driver. They ride without seat belts, the better to hasten their exit if a blowout looms. Truck-enveloping breaks in the ice are rare these days, though. Companies use ground-penetrating radar that can measure the thickness of the ice to within three centimetres, although it's been said there is no substitute for testing with an auger and measuring tape. A few trucks have met icy demises, but the considerable time lag between the moment of their hasty abandonment and their full submersion has allowed many drivers to escape. Falling in, even if you get out, is not advisable. The estimated survival time of a wet person at minus-forty Celsius – a not-uncommon extreme – is fifteen minutes.

The ice has its moods. With no heed to the wheels of the rolling behemoths, it heaves and contracts, sending so-called pressure ridges of concrete-dense obstacles jutting from the surface or exposing two-foot chasms of black water. The ice groans like a bandaged patient. It cracks like distant thunder. Some drivers turn up music to block out the noise. Alden is among those drivers.

"When you pull up to a lake and you hear the ice crack and everything's going great, you play the same tune all the way across," he says. "When you do that, there's nothing to worry about."

In the check-in trailer, the departure hour is drawing nearer. The clerk in charge of dispatching the trucks at regular intervals says there are five minutes to go, but now there was another visitor. A man with a digital video camera jokingly introduces himself to the clerk as Dan Rather. He wants a moment to speak with the drivers for a documentary he is pitching to a cable TV specialty channel. The clerk, a young woman, is not impressed.

"Hey, Dan Rather," she says. "You've got one minute."

The man with the camera asks the truckers what makes their job worth doing.

"The ice road's a bug," says Alden.

And tonight the bug will be buzzing.

The road begins as a paved-and-gravel track that winds from the outskirts of Yellowknife to the edge of a lake. At the lake's sloping shoreline, in the chill of the winter months, big trucks point their noses down a bank and begin their slow creep across the frozen water toward the mines.

Most residents of Yellowknife rolled their eyes in the 1980s, when they heard prospectors were scouring the tundra in a desperate search for diamonds. It wasn't that the Subarctic and Arctic didn't have a history of mineral richness. The uranium that was the raw material for the first atomic bombs was plucked from the Eldorado mine, which opened in the 1930s nearly five hundred kilometres northwest of the city on the shore of Great Bear Lake. Not far from there the Echo Bay mine produced high-grade silver between 1965 and 1975, all of which led to the expansion of a settlement that was named capital of the Northwest Territories in 1967. The discovery of the Giant Mine, a large deposit that would yield 220,000 kilograms of gold from its 1948 opening to its 2004 closing, spurred a rush of post-war prospecting and left behind the detritus of gold mining's nasty side: tonnes of arsenic trioxide, a poisonous by-product of the gold-extraction process that seeps into groundwater during thaws and offers no cheap cleanup.

Yellowknife knew gold, but diamonds were an off-the-radar concern, even if searching for them wasn't necessarily new. Geologists from De Beers, the South African company that has long been the world's biggest seller of diamonds, thought highly enough of the conditions in Canadian bedrock that the company began quietly staking claims as early as the 1960s. But false alarms weren't new in the diamond-prospecting business. Jacques Cartier, the great explorer of the 1500s, thought he'd stumbled upon a fortune when he picked up what looked like a diamond on the shore of the St. Lawrence River. The stone turned out to be quartz, and thus was born a French saying – "*voilà un diamant du Canada*," or fake as a Canadian diamond in the translation – that endured for centuries.

But there was nothing fake about the hard work of geologists Chuck Fipke and his prospecting partner Stu Blusson. In 1985, after years of northerly toil, Fipke found what he was convinced was evidence of the presence of diamonds near Lac de Gras, about three hundred kilometres northeast of Yellowknife, about two hundred kilometres south of the Arctic Circle. He wasn't wrong. When the discovery of diamonds in the Subarctic was announced in 1991, it set off a frenzy of claim-staking that was unprecedented in North America. Two decades later, the Ekati mine is a seven-year-old money machine, generating some US$2.8 billion in revenue as of 2005.

In 1994, the diamonds at the Diavik mine were found beneath Lac de Gras, so they drained the lake. It took millions of tonnes of stone to build the first dike, the A 154, which extends nearly four kilometres and cordons off a 1.5-square-kilometre area that, once the dike was watertight, in July 2002, took three months to drain. The dike, an average of ten metres high, twenty-eight metres at its high point, took two years to build. Another dike, the A 418, was under construction as of this writing. It is shorter by comparison, just 1.3 kilometres long, but will be built in water up to thirty-two metres deep.

The diamonds themselves are found in kimberlite pipes. Kimberlite, named for the South African town, Kimberly, where it was first noted, is the product of volcanic eruptions that happened 110 million to 20 million years ago. Magma, or molten rock, was pushed from as much as two hundred kilometres below the earth's surface through fractures that acted as conduits. As the magma rose, it pushed rocks and minerals, including diamonds, to the surface. When the magma cooled, it left behind carrot-shaped veins of kimberlite that contained diamonds. The pipes at the Diavik mine, which number sixty-four, are some of the highest-grade in the world. Typically, diamond miners will have to harvest one tonne of rock to yield one carat of diamonds. Diavik's ratio has been estimated at approximately three carats per tonne.

Every day workers move ninety thousand tonnes of rock. Every day thousands of carats of rough diamonds are extracted through a process that uses none of the toxic substances that make gold mining so lamentable. Once the kimberlite is harvested and brought to the production facility in dump trucks three storeys high, it is crushed and eventually fed onto conveyor belts where the diamonds are finally separated from the worthless rubble. When diamonds are exposed to X-rays, they fluoresce – that is, they emit electromagnetic radiation in the form of visible light. Photo-electric sensors detect this and, in turn, trip a machine that produces a small blast of air that blows the diamond from the conveyor into a receptacle. The diamonds are then shipped to a facility in Yellowknife where they are cleaned and divided and evaluated for government-royalty calculations.

The Northwest Territories' gross domestic product is, thanks in large part to the effects of the Diavik and Ekati mines, growing about 10 per cent every year – more than five times the national average. The profits are staggering.

BHP Billiton, the Australian mining company that owns 80 per cent of the Ekati mine (Fipke and Blusson own the other 20 per cent) is said to make an 80 per cent return on its investment in the Ekati mine. Toronto-based Aber Diamond Corp., which has a 40 per cent stake in the Diavik mine, reported a quarterly profit of $13.6 million in April of 2005, a more than fourfold year-over-year increase. The rest of Diavik is owned by London-based Rio Tinto Group, the world's third-largest mining interest.

The mine's physical plant is astounding. There are three 18-million-litre diesel fuel tanks that provide the juice for everything from power generation and heating to trucks and diggers and the like. There is a mile-long gravel runway that can safely accommodate jets as large as the Boeing 737, not to mention Hercules transport planes. There is a sewage treatment plant for the seven-hundred-odd employees. Over at the Ekati mine, they boast of squash courts and putting greens and golf-course simulators for employee recreation. Expense isn't exactly spared.

But demand for diamonds is high enough – an $11 billion annual global market – that there are plenty of companies willing to take the risk of prospecting for the elusive gems. In 2005, there were some sixty firms spending millions to scour the Arctic for strikes akin to Diavik and Ekati. Those two mines alone turned Canada into the third-largest producer of raw diamonds in the world. But finding a similar mother lode is unlikely. There have been some seven thousand kimberlite pipes discovered around the world, but only 15 per cent of those have actually reaped diamonds, and less than 1 per cent bear enough sparkling fruit to warrant the construction of a major mine. Upon striking kimberlite, it can take years to do the proper tests to establish whether the pipe is economically feasible.

Patience can pay off. The South African mines that made De Beer's a global force have nearly been picked clean. The world's biggest diamond mine, the Argyle in northern Australia, is set to close in 2007. Fipke, whose strike at Ekati has made him one of Canada's one hundred wealthiest people with assets of about $341 million according to *Canadian Business* magazine's 2004 Rich List, has moved on to Angola, the former Portuguese colony in southwest Africa, which is already the world's fourth-largest diamond producer and, after decades of civil war, has been characterized by experts as largely unexplored.

"We're hoping to make an Ekati-style discovery there," Fipke told Bloomberg News in 2005.

Diavik's diamonds are expected to last for at least a couple of decades. In 1999, Tiffany and Co., the New York City jeweller, made an agreement with Aber to buy at least $50 million in diamonds annually for ten years. The company, the first retailer to buy gems straight from a mine, opened a cutting and polishing facility near the Yellowknife airport in 2003. Workers are flown in on air taxis, staying on site for two weeks before flying home for two weeks off. Some 40 per cent of the workers at both mines are aboriginal. The average salary for workers employed by the diamond mines from 1998 to 2001 was $61,639, according to Statistics Canada.

It's tough to calculate the average salary for an ice-road trucker. As independent owner-operators, their economics are their own business. How much they make depends on a handful of factors, including the fuel efficiency of their truck, the affordability of their truck's financing, not to mention their will to keep driving. Alden, for his part, is currently relishing the driving on the road before the ice road, an old-fashioned, dry-land sidewinder that slithers and curls into the night. Perhaps because he will soon be restricted to trolling at 25 km/h, he attacks the rolling hills by standing on his accelerator. When he prepares to wrap his eighty-four-foot speedster around a coming curve, he preludes the turn with anticipatory play-by-play.

"You like roller coasters?" he says, approaching a hard left. "This, you're gonna enjoy. This is just a basic switchback. If I didn't have a big load on like that and I was in front, I'd make it just tickle."

We are at the turn's apex. The truck, labouring on a slight uphill, is wheezing.

"Feel this puppy?" says Alden.

"Yeah," I say. But I can't feel a thing, to be honest, save for the jostle of the potholes and the throaty vibration of the engine. Out the window, the boreal forest is zipping by at eighty kilometres an hour, the trees disappearing into the darkness behind our passing headlights. Up ahead, Alden points out the V Lake Curve. It is, he says, a "doozy."

"You're going to feel some shit going on that you're not going to like. You can take a corner at a fairly good clip as long as you don't, say, slow down after you get into it.

Because it's like physics – the inertia will pile up behind you. As long as you sustain your speed, you're all right."

Alden has sustained his nine-year northerly career longer than any of Robinson's drivers save one. His rare longevity speaks to what Alden calls the "burnout rate." For many, the ice roads are a one-winter fling. Single men miss civilization's comforts; Colin isn't sure if he'll be returning next year because, he's told his father, it's difficult to build a life around a two-month job.

Married men lament the absence of their wives. Gary, Alden tells me, is currently fighting a particularly nasty bout of homesickness. "He's missing Momma pretty good right now," says Alden.

Alden's bride of twenty-three years is represented in the cab by a cellphone dangling by its power cord from the dash. She calls most days. They miss each other. "But we've got a pretty good arrangement," he says.

Alden's enthusiasm for the road, meanwhile, borders on the fanatic. For years he's been preserving many of his runs on video, Velcroing his hand-held camera to the dashboard and letting it roll across the white-on-white landscape in both moonlight and sun. "I just make sure my window's clean," he laughs. Other than professional athletes and entertainers, I can't think of an occupation in which a worker would feel the need to videotape his day's work for posterity. I ask him why he does this.

"There's three kinds of jobs," he says, shifting down into another sharp turn, shifting his weight with the curve as though he were driving a go-kart. "The first kind, the people are good, the job's no good. The second kind, the job's good, but the people are no good. And the third kind, that's what I've got here."

A little farther down the road, Alden adds: "And, you know, it beats working in a factory."

"It beats working in a factory" is the trucker's worldwide refrain. Since I have never been a trucker, I cannot speak to its veracity. But I can speak to this: Everything, in my experience, beats working in a factory. I have worked my share of chump jobs, stocking shelves, stuffing envelopes, sorting cases of skunky, cigarette-filled beer bottles. But never have I rued the beginning of a shift more than I rued the beginning of a shift during two summers spent slogging in an auto-parts factory. Part of the reason I hated the place was that it scared me. The week before I got the gig, one of the full-time regulars lost a couple of fingers when the machine on which he was putting in his eight hours – an ancient, two-storey unit that cut brake drums – failed, sending a few thousand pounds of cast-iron mechanism collapsing on his hand. A couple of weeks later, I was manning the very same model of machine, attempting to calculate the statistical probability of two finger-chopping calamities in one summer. In the end, when I took into account the half-century-old machinery and the alarming frequency of less dramatic system failures that left work stations out of commission for days, I concluded the probability was pretty darn high.

If my math was fuzzy, it was because the place was literally a sweatshop. I would change my T-shirt four times a

shift, but the exercise was futile. In the oppressive humidity of a Southern Ontario summer – in a building filled
with machines that used toxic baths of fluid to lubricate
and cool the machining process, which in turn got hot and
expelled a steamy mist that formed a ceiling-high haze –
my cotton shirts would only stay dry for a few moments.

It was exhausting. On one of my first days, I stretched
out on the factory's front lawn after I had finished lunch,
and I was awakened by the scowling foreman, who shook
me by the shoulders and said, "Do you want to make money,
or do you want to drool?" I had many conversations with
the lifers, strong men whose labour was making them
weaker. They would invariably put a hand on my shoulder
and say some version of: "Whatever you do, son, stay in
school." A few years after I left that factory for the last time,
its doors closed and its workers were displaced. I never
missed it.

Alden gets a hankering for winter-road hauling around
the time the first snowflake falls in a Saskatchewan autumn.
He's a rare devotee. Driver turnover is high. The work is
stressful and seasonal. It's non-stop for two months then
it's full stop.

"Jim Langel's the only trucker on the road who's been
here longer than me," he says. "He's been here since 1989.
People come and they go. A lot of people come and have
a look and they don't make the money they want or they
have a bad year. People change. Things are going on in your
life. But this is a very good job for a lot of people to come
and work from seven weeks, eight weeks. You see some

things you never seen before. You make a couple of bucks. You go home, tell your buddies. It's great.

"When I came here, there was sixty, seventy trucks. Now, with the diamond mines, there's five hundred. You knew everybody back then. It was different. Now there's too many people. Even I'm getting tired of it."

The drivers have been coming in greater numbers because diamonds have become a more lucrative industry than most locals ever dreamed. The local government has trademarked the phrase "Diamond Capital of the World" and printed it on the lamppost flags that flank some of Yellowknife's downtown streets. The territory's economy grew 19.2 per cent in 2001; the rest of the country settled for 1.5 per cent in growth. The population is at an all-time high of eighteen thousand. Per capita income is the highest of any city in Canada. The unemployment rate was among the lowest in Canada. A three-bedroom trailer on a sliver of real estate can cost as much as $180,000. The federal government could earn as much as $7.5 billion in royalties from the Ekati, Diavik, and Snap Lake mines, the latter of which is expected to be operational in 2007, during their two-decade existences. The territory will get some $260 million, although it has lobbied for more to cover infrastructure costs.

But the territorial government's case isn't clear-cut. Said Eira Thomas, the geologist credited with finding the Diavik mine, "You don't need a lot of infrastructure. Basically, you can fly out a week's production in a briefcase."

Seasonal truckers, with their beds on wheels, never had to worry about a place to stay, which made their overhead attractively low and ice-road trucking impressively lucrative. Alden breaks down the numbers for me. In the five weeks since Alden and Colin rolled into camp, they've made fourteen trips to the mine. They made, as a two-truck tandem, $7,000 each trip. Each trip cost them $2,200 in combined fuel. And that left them with a $4,800 profit on each outing, which, when you figure that each round trip took in the neighbourhood of forty-eight hours, worked out to fifty dollars an hour apiece.

That's good money made even better by the fact that there is no cost to sleep and eat. The food in the Robinson kitchen and at Lockhart Camp is free. Most of the trucks have double bunks tucked behind the seats. And there are barracks, too, at Robinson's Yellowknife compound if a driver feels the need for respite from the omnipresent growl of diesel engines.

Alden laughs when I ask if he is getting enough sleep. We have just arrived at the entrance to the first lake on the ice road, and my chauffeur is inching his Western Star onto the ice.

"I'll sleep when I get home," he says, and by that he means Saskatchewan in six weeks.

As he speaks I catch my first glimpse of the white plain of ice that facilitates the relatively cheap transport of supplies to the burgeoning mines, not to mention the kind of heavy equipment that couldn't be transported by air even if cost permitted, which – because plane shipments are prohibitively expensive – it doesn't. Before us lies a vast expanse of snow. In the light of Alden's headlights, in the light of the moon, I see moonscape contours. I see drifts and truck tracks. And I see a perfectly plowed thorough-fare, the width of perhaps a dozen lanes of traffic on more southerly roads, lined by tidy banks of snow heaped by passing plows. I hear a crackle when tires meet ice, like cellophane being ripped from a fruit basket.

It's a shocking sound for a neophyte, surely the sound, one first thinks, of the great lake preparing to swallow this rig and these men and their cargo into its evil jaws of ice. But perhaps my night-table reading was far too fresh in my mind. The book was *Denison's Ice Road*, Edith Iglauer's 1974 account of the building of an ice road from the edge of Yellowknife to the Echo Bay silver mine. John Denison, a Mountie who quit the police force because he said he got squeamish on the scene of traffic fatalities, first cleared a trail from Yellowknife north in the 1960s, losing at least five men in eight winters' work. Denison had been spearhead-ing the road to the silver mine since 1964, when equipment was inferior and winters were colder and the construction of the road wasn't aided by the availability of a road crew that was equipped, as are the crews of today, with portable workshops and generators and welders, not to mention a food supply to sustain a thirty-day mission. In Denison's day, he didn't have satellite phones and scout aircraft. He had an auger and a feeling. And sometimes neither helped much. Trucks in his construction convoy crashed through the ice more than once on Iglauer's journey.

As Iglauer wrote: "The North grips a man; the space, the quiet, the feeling of being a pioneer gets to him. The men who began driving for Denison still come back year after year to make the dangerous run he carved out for them. Their over-sized trailer trucks carry everything from tractors to peanuts, refrigerators, mine machinery, cribbage boards, heavy steel beams, small pickup trucks, groceries, beer, propane gas, lumber, fuel drums, crude ore in dull grey bags, or a million and a half dollars worth of 'jig,' silver ore so high grade it is shipped out rough-crushed in a sealed van. A lonely, hazardous trip, even in convoy. A driver usually can see the truck behind him in his side mirror or watch the massive vehicle ahead of him move safely across a lake and fight its way up the incline of the next portage, but something in his own truck may snap any time in the brittle cold; or he can misjudge a curve in the road or a snowbank and overturn; or on the lake that the truck ahead just crossed safely, he can plunge to the bottom. On the Ice Road, especially when crossing the lakes, a driver keeps one hand on the steering wheel and the other on the handle of the door nearest him, which he may already have left ajar on the second latch. When a driver and his truck run out of ice it's time to jump and every second counts."

I knew Alden was right: The risk was minimal, nearly non-existent. Still, I thought of those words as I inched a hand toward my door handle. Alden, oblivious to my brief bout of nervousness, was speaking.

"Diamonds were starting out in '94, but everybody was laughing at them. 'Diamonds in Canada? Who's heard of that?' But I wish I'd invested my money," Alden says, launching into a story about his rookie season in these parts. "We did things then that they wouldn't even consider now. It was expansion, you know? We were out there trying to get these machines going. I've done more in my fuckin' life up here than most people will do in three lifetimes. I've seen shit up here – and in no way have I seen some of the shit some people have seen – but I've done some things nobody else has done. Most of the adventures and great times in my life happened here.

"If it was just a job, you wouldn't put your full energy into it. This is me. This is what I do. It has soul and it has character."

We are arriving at the Meadows, a staging area where trucks line up and wait for clearance from the road's security detail. It is 10:17 p.m. We are 258 kilometres south of Diavik mine, Alden's destination, and 271 kilometres south of Ekati mine. And now, after an affirmative word on the CB from Wally, the pickup-truck-driving security chief, we are finally on the move, northward.

I learn a lot about Alden and the ice road in the next six hours. I learn that his favourite movie is *Ghost*, with Demi Moore and Whoopi Goldberg; that he isn't a very big fan of the Vietnamese chef at the Robinson kitchen ("You don't get an hour out of town and you're hungry again"); and that he has a theory on almost everything. He has a theory, for instance, on car-truck crashes and why the cars rarely escape without, at the very least, a caved-in flank.

"Say, for instance, you make a mistake on the highway," he says, addressing me as the theoretical motorist. "If you're spinning out in front of me and I turn the wheel, I'm fucked. Because maybe, when the dust settles, you're goin' down the highway and I'm looking at my jack-knifed tractor-trailer. And I say to the police, 'Well, this guy did this in front of me.' And they say, 'Where is he? Prove it.' It's a phantom crash, right? I'm supposed to take a piece of you. I'm supposed to get some paint. People don't know that, but it's true."

And he has a rule of thumb on avoiding broken noses.

"Remember this," he tells me when we get talking, for whatever reason, about fist fighting. "If somebody's going to get in a fight and they're standing there yakking at you, if they were gonna hit you, they woulda done it already. If they had the intention of stickin' you with a knife, they woulda already done it. Now, there's negotiations. They will always leave you a way out. Just back up and say, 'I'm in the wrong place.'"

Sometime after he utters those last words, Alden nudges me awake. It is well past 2 a.m., and the sameness of the scenery – the blurry whiteness of the road only interrupted by the hazy approach of a southbound truck's headlights – has been conspiring to lower my eyelids for most of the past hour. Alden suggests I apply eye drops. I comply, no easy feat in the bouncing cab, and the Visine also finds a home in my mouth and in my right ear. But the lubricating effect in my eyes only seems to facilitate my droop. I finally take Alden up on his offer and submit to top-bunk lay-down. Twenty-three minutes later I awake refreshed. And when I stumble back into the passenger seat – as the pace crawls to 15 km/h on Flo's Lake, southbound traffic coming more frequently now – I see, to my delight, the fuzzy luminescence of the northern lights.

The sight of the morphing waves of light, which I haven't seen since I was a child at a Northern Ontario cottage, jolts me further awake. Aurora borealis bursts through the scattered clouds like a neon green arrow, like alarm-clock numbers in your bedroom. Alden yawns loud and long.

"If the moon wasn't out you'd really see some shit," he says. But the moon and the stars, when they emerge from behind a few translucent clouds, seem to explode at this latitude. We advance in silence for a long moment. The chatter on the CB, incessant for most of the evening, has mostly stopped and when someone deems to speak, they do so in a hushed tone, church-appropriate.

Alden yawns again. It's past 3 a.m.; then it's 3:30, and I keep my eyes on the green lights on the horizon, now trans-forming into the shape of a perfect check mark, previously entangled in a yin-yang fetal curl.

"I want a day off so bad I could puke for it," Alden says as the clock strikes four. "I mean, I put 'em all to bed" – he's speaking of the other drivers – "I put 'em all to bed. And I don't take nothing. Just a little water, coffee, an aspirin to cut the tension."

"It's all up here." He points to his temple. "But I haven't had a day off since February 2nd." It is March 14.

We are reaching my drop-off point, and I am regretting my visit's bad timing. Because of the restriction on daytime travel, Janet Robinson surmised that my three-night stay in Yellowknife wouldn't allow for a return trip to the mine. In lieu, I am being paired with a south-heading driver whose path will be crossing Alden's in about fifteen minutes.

We say our goodbyes. I thank him for his hospitality, and he asks me to guess how far we'd travelled from Yellowknife. I say 160 kilometres; he fusses with the buttons on his GPS, and, after some cursing, announces the actual number was 154. "Fuck, are you ever good," he says.

I shake his hand and hop out the door into the blowing cold, the road's surface crunching beneath my feet as I make the fifty-metre jog to the lane bound for Yellowknife. Julian Barre is idling in wait.

Julian is wearing a T-shirt and stocking feet, the heels of his white sweat socks resting on a folded square of paper towel that he occasionally adjusts to maintain a buffer from the wet floor mat. He hails from Calgary, where downtime in his job in the construction industry coincides ideally with the ice-road season. This is his fourth Yellowknife winter.

"My wife often said I can never be anything but a truck

driver," he says. "Because I can sit here, going sixty kilometres an hour across this lake, going 1,200 rpm, and just listen to the engine."

He is allowed to go sixty kilometres an hour across this lake because his 425-horsepower Kenworth T-2000, with which he'd hauled steel rods to the mine, is empty save for the contents of his cab, which includes a box of cassette tapes with vintages ranging, by my count, from 1975 to 1983.

At 5:21 a.m., as slivers of dawn pierce the clouds in the eastern sky, Julian opens the box and pushes it my way. I insist he choose the tunes. He covers a yawn with his right hand and makes his selection.

"When a person starts to get tired, you put in some Headpins or Judas Priest – something a little lively," he says. Headpins, a Vancouver heavy-metal band formed in 1982, get the nod. Their crunchy growl on Julian's rig's system sounds, in a word, nasal. Their lyrics are repetitive enough for me to take notes.

"You keep pluggin' away!" the singer screeches. And Julian does, indeed. He has been up here since November, helping stockpile fuel in Yellowknife before the weather got bad.

"I had a small bowl of patience for breakfast this morning," he says when I ask him how he keeps going. "Some guys just don't get it. It doesn't work like a Swiss watch up here. But this job gives you a lot of time to pay attention to the simple things: the sunrise, the sunset, a lot of things you don't pay attention to when you're in the city. As monotonous as this job can be, it takes a lot of patience.

It gets a little harder every year. That's why you need a good
supply of music and a good book or two."

Four nights before, Julian squeezed in plenty of reading
when a storm made visibility nil and the road turned into a
twelve-hour parking lot. He read Jack Adrian's *Deathlands*,
a science-fiction novel complete with mutants and a nuclear
winter. He says he reads a lot of science fiction.

It is past 6 a.m. To our right, near the waist-high bank
of snow that marks the road's western extreme, we see a
gang of ravens picking at a carcass. "Caribou," said Julian.
We see laconic white doves sitting in the middle of the road
despite our pending presence, not moving until Julian's
horn inspires them to scatter. We pass, too, one last convoy
of northbound traffic, this one carrying a so-called rock
box, the massive cargo hold of mining's version of a dump
truck. The sky is rising like a pale red curtain; the sun is
starting to make us squint. In a couple of hours we'll be
back on asphalt. Julian pushes a button to remove the tape
from its player. We have been listening to the Headpins
play for more than two hours, and now we stop.

"Quite a bit involved, eh?" he says, "just for digging up
shiny little stones for your fiancée."

But on a gentle day like this, I am thinking of my
intrepid predecessors on this journey – men like John
Denison. Back then, trucks frequently broke down in the
chill, grizzly bears raided food-storage shacks. The fron-
tier was wild and deadly. And Denison seemed crazy for
his trouble.

"No one else wanted to do this job, so I said, 'Why not?'" he once said. "Anyway, I like doin' it, and if I lie down and quit, I might as well have never started."

Technology can't stop winter, maybe – although there are people convinced it is shortening it – but technology has removed most of winter's perils. These massive rigs and their computer-controlled engines, satellites, cell-phones, and CBs – none of these things have tamed the conditions alone, but they've removed their sting.

As Julian motors into Yellowknife's outskirts, as he hops out of his truck at the Nuna Logistics trailer to announce his arrival in a T-shirt and a half-slipped-on pair of boots, I laugh. Winter in the north, indeed, is going south.

"This is city driving," Dick Robinson, the patriarch of the Robinson enterprise, whose ice-road trucking operation made him a multi-millionaire from a stake of $15,000 in 1969, once said. "Next year I'll come up in my Lincoln, to show the boys it's not such a hardship after all."

Alas, just when it seems like driving the ice isn't such a hardship; just when it seems like nature's been tamed by science and ambition and the gravity of money, it isn't. A couple of winters after my trip, Dick Robinson's grandson, Gary, would die while preparing a road for heavy use on Prosperous Lake. He was in a snowplow in the late days of December, before most of the truck drivers arrive for the hauling season. According to a report, divers arrived on the scene some thirty minutes after he disappeared, but to no avail. He was twenty-three.

How did something so catastrophic happen in an era in which the ice thickness is monitored by sophisticated equipment?

"The truth is they lost respect for the ice," says Alden, offering his opinion over the line from Saskatchewan. "They were using the wrong truck. It was too short and too heavy. It was a most unfortunate incident and it did not have to happen . . .

"You see, when most people drive on the ice, the danger part is past. They don't see the ice at its beginning and a lot of them are gone home by the time it starts to deteriorate. On the day Gary went through, they shouldn't have been there. They were a little early . . . The theory is that the sooner you get out there and get the snow off, the better ice you're going to get, the earlier you're going to get [trucks on] the ice. And there was a bit of a push.

"They forgot that maybe it can hurt you bad. It's the idea that they had become so complacent. Nobody'd been hurt. Nobody'd got wet. And then this."

Plowing the ice roads has never been a glamorous gig. You're driving on virgin ice, and you're also pushing snow from northern lakes whose surfaces are often broken up by the tips of protruding rocks, few of which can be seen beneath a layer of white.

"It isn't if you're going to hit a rock, it's when you're going to hit it," Alden says. "Even on lakes you've been on lots of times, it's bound to happen. The last person to get hurt, I guess, was me. I smoked a rock pretty bad. The plow busted up. I went to sleep for a moment or two. It's just like a full-fledged crash, the only difference is because the plow's on an angle, you divert to one side instead of hitting head-on. You go from full throttle to dead stop. I was plowing through the narrows at a place called King Lake. I didn't see it coming."

Marvin Robinson, Gary's father, didn't respond to requests for an interview. But at least a couple of ice-road truckers suggested the ever-shrinking ice-road season – a result of global warming – was as much a culprit as anything. Global warming is changing the way some of the residents of the north look at transportation. There is talk of building a $700-million highway to connect Tuktoyaktuk, a port of 930 people on the oil- and gas-laden Beaufort Sea, to Canada's highway system. Currently Tuktoyaktuk can be reached only by ice roads, by barge, or by plane, which makes the cost of living exorbitant – a two-litre bottle of pop can go for as much as ten dollars. But now that the ice-road window has narrowed, there is an increasing urge to find another way. There are those who believe a dry-land road to the Beaufort, an idea which has been bandied about since the 1950s, has become viable with the ever-rising demand – and escalating price – of energy.

"We're already connected from sea to sea as a country," Joe Handley, the premier of the Northwest Territories, has said. "What this would do is connect us from sea to sea to sea. The time has come to finish this."

But all-weather roads have been built before at such rare latitudes, and with not-so-booming results. The Dempster Highway, which connects Dempster Corner,

Yukon, and Inuvik, NWT, is the first Canadian highway to cross the Arctic Circle. The lonely strip of gravel was conceived in the late 1950s as part of prime minister John Diefenbaker's plan to more efficiently exploit the north's resources, but it wasn't officially opened until 1979, when oil drilling in the Beaufort made it more economically viable. It has attracted at least one certifiable eccentric: Harry Waldron, the self-proclaimed "Keeper of the Arctic Circle," became well known for sitting in a rocking chair at the highway's edge, wearing a tuxedo and sipping champagne. Some days he'd hand out proclamations to travellers to authenticate their trip across the Arctic Circle. It has also attracted truckers disenchanted with the daily grind of the continent's economic hubs.

"I couldn't handle the Montreal-Toronto run every day. It's much too boring," one Dempster Highway trucker told the *Globe and Mail* in 1987. "Up here, there is something new and interesting every day. If it isn't a grizzly chasing and taking a swipe with his paw at half-wild horses at full gallop, it's a whiteout with visibility reduced to absolutely zero, or a ninety-six-year-old Indian out for a walk in the middle of the road at two in the morning in the dead of winter."

Alden, for his part, might be finished with ice-road driving. It's the summer following his fourteenth year on the ice, and he's found work in a new diamond mine – this one just a half-hour drive from his homestead in Smeaton. The mine is still in its exploratory phase, and Alden, as an employee who works, not in a truck, but in the part of the operation where the actual extraction of minerals takes place, has signed a confidentiality agreement and is sworn to secrecy about the prospects. But he can't conceal his optimism.

"This is going to be the new boomtown of the Canadian north," he says. "It had gotten to the point where the farming's all dried up and everybody's piss broke. And now we've got this.

"I'm not sure I'm going back north again."

Still, though he says he has shares in the company that's prospecting for bling, his trucking career might not yet be complete. He needs to sell his truck for a decent price – about fifty thousand dollars, he figures – or he may be forced by economic necessity to return to Yellowknife at the top of the new year. With fuel prices as high as they are, though, he's not optimistic about finding a buyer.

"Anybody who's trucking around here has got a job because somebody's cut the rates so bad nobody else wants it," he says. "If I can't sell my truck for what I want for it, I'm going to go north one more time. It's about money. It's about paying the bills. It's about getting what you need out of it. But on the thirty-first of August, my wife, Jill, and I, we were married thirty-one years. Fourteen of those years I was gone to Yellowknife for the winter, and every other winter I've worked away. Every time you leave home it takes a little chip out of you.

"But as far as driving being lonely or desolate, I never thought of it that way, because you're around some people . . . Drive down the freeway and break down. That's lonely.

You might as well be up in the barrenlands. People don't stop. They don't give a shit. When I go up north, I'm with some people who I would and they would put their life on the line to help me. They don't come better. A job doesn't come any better."

4

Too Many Doughnuts

Dave and I are sitting in the cab of his Mack truck in Hamilton, Ontario, preparing to haul cargo to Buffalo before dawn on a frigid January morning. I am bundled in a scarf and a parka, grey work socks, and flannel-lined boots. Dave, who is fifty-seven years old, is wearing a short-sleeved purple polo shirt beneath thread-bare coveralls beneath a black fleece sweatshirt that is hanging open around his beach-ball-sized belly. But he does not appear to feel the cold. I, on the other hand, am freezing, mostly because Dave's door is open and the frequent gusts of crosswind pepper us with the ice pellets that have been lubricating the roads for the past hour. Dave notices me shivering and finally yanks his door shut. And although the two-seater cab is closed to the elements, we are not alone. On the dusty plastic dashboard, underneath a switch labelled "Mirror Heat," there hangs a postcard-sized calendar. Miss January gazes back at us from a seaside vista, busty and shirtless, her long fingernails fondling her navel. Dave catches me making notes on these details and laughs. "Ah," he says, "she keeps me young."

He reaches into the deep pockets of his coveralls and pulls out two cellphones. One is the size of a brick, a decade-old dinosaur. "That's if they want to get a hold of you," he says, motioning toward his dispatcher's office. The other phone, which he lays in a tray behind the steering wheel, looks to have been manufactured more recently. "That's if the wife wants to get a hold of you . . . which she always does."

Dave works for a company called Fluke Transport, so the back of his truck bears a slogan that's well known in these parts. The slogan is: "If it's on time, it's a Fluke." And the same self-deprecating wit is evident in Dave's early-morning chatter. His job is nothing like that of the long-haul truckers with whom I'll be sharing most of my travels. He works 5 a.m. until 2 p.m., rarely travels farther than two hundred miles from home, and sleeps in his own bed every night. "It's sissy work," he says with a smile. And while he later acknowledges that it's an enviable gig – that few of his peers get the privilege of 365 nights per annum in their own bed – jobs like this don't come to the inexperienced. Before this, he logged more than twenty years and 2.5 million miles as a cross-country hauler, delivering fresh Chryslers all over the United States and Canada, so he knows his trade, and he has fallen prey to one of its major occupation hazards. Truckers, it's no secret, are an unhealthy lot. The life expectancy of a white male who spends two decades in the long-distance business has been estimated at sixty-six, seven years fewer than the North American average. And Dave almost didn't make it to fifty-six. He had a heart attack at the wheel last year. Although he fell unconscious by the end of his ordeal, he managed to steer his truck to the shoulder while he simultaneously clutched at his chest and dialled 9-1-1 on his late-model cellphone.

He underwent angioplasty to clear a couple of blocked arteries. And ever since he's been attempting not to clog his remaining vessels. Still, not long after he turns the key and the Mack rumbles to life, we are twenty miles down the highway and pulling into the Donut Diner, where we back into a parking lot jammed with rigs. The teenaged girl behind the counter immediately pours my companion a coffee, and then adds a single packet of sweetener and a dollop of skim milk.

"He's payin'," says Dave, motioning my way.

I ask Dave if he'd like a doughnut – although as soon as I utter the words I realize fried sugar isn't exactly a heart-healthy choice – but the girl behind the counter answers for him.

"He's not allowed," she says, reaching over the counter to offer a playful slap of a regular's hand.

Dave shakes his head and mumbles, "Ah, she's right. I'm all healthy now. It sucks."

I order black coffee and we're away. From the outskirts of Toronto, where we are currently parked, it'll be an hour's drive south into Western New York, where an ice storm has knocked out the power and felled trees are lining the

roads. We stop at the Queenston-Lewiston border crossing, where the U.S. guard knows Dave's face and motions
him to drive through.

"They don't care about a guy like me," Dave says. "They
pull over one guy with two hundred pounds of dope, three
other guys are squeezing into the country behind him."

Indeed, I've been witness to at least one distracting to-
do at the border: A couple of years back, I drove a convert-
ible from Toronto to Buffalo with the Stanley Cup, hockey's
greatest prize, strapped into the passenger seat. It was a
stunt in the name of a story for the *National Post*, the
Toronto daily newspaper at which I worked. I posed for
pictures with what seemed like every border guard on duty;
even the American officers were smitten by the Cup's glow.
I can only guess at the volume of vice that used my presence as a smokescreen.

It is fitting that we are hauling a trailer-load of wool
bound for the shelves of America's Wal-Marts, because in
those sixty minutes, over the considerable wheezing of a
thirteen-speed engine and the incessant chatter on the
CB, Dave weaves some lengthy yarns. He talks of the time
he yanked a woman and her ten-year-old daughter out of
a Colorado gorge in sub-zero weather. (He saw their car
swerve through a guardrail, then lowered himself into their
landing area with his truck's winch.) He tells of his own
brush with death, when he averted a head-on crash with a
trucker who had fallen asleep at the wheel by zigzagging his
rig through a maze of telephone polls and oak trees, then
bringing it to an improbable stop just a few feet from the

bank of a tributary of the Mississippi River. But mostly he discusses his battle with the bulge. He has lost twenty-three pounds in the past eleven months. He stands five-foot-nine and weighs 234, but his doctor wants him to lose four pounds per month for the next year, bringing him closer to his high-school weight of 180. He is doubting his willpower.

"It's tough to stay fit out here," he says. "Junk food's everywhere. And I love junk food."

We make it to Buffalo and back without hitting a drive-thru. We drop off the wool, pick up a load of recycled cardboard, and we're home just past noon. Dave's day, save for a mound of paperwork he'll complete before heading out, is done.

Not far up the highway from the warehouse where I leave Dave, the line of trucks crawls slowly by the window, a stream of groaning, bouncing metal beasts that never really abates. Sitting in the inspection station on a westbound stretch of the Queen Elizabeth Way, Jax, one of Ontario's three-hundred-some transportation enforcement officers – one of the banes of North American truckers' existence – gazes out at the flow and sighs.

"Rush hour," says Jax, "seems to be 24-7 these days."

The United States does 2 million random roadside inspections every year, 20 per cent of which result in rigs being ordered off the road for safety violations, 8 per cent of which nab truckers for falsifying logbooks or for being considered "unfit" to drive.

"Can you imagine if we allowed an airline to fly if 20 per cent of its planes were not airworthy, 10 per cent of its pilots shouldn't be flying, and they had fifteen or twenty accidents in the past year," Kenneth Mead, the U.S. Department of Transportation's inspector general, has said. Enforcement ebbs and flows with the times. The average fine in the United States for a truck safety violation fell from $3,700 in 1995 to $1,600 in 2000. And in 89 per cent of serious safety cases, truckers weren't fined anything.

Jax sits by a computer screen that tells her the weight of each of the truck's axles. The technology makes spotting overweight trucks a cinch, but there's more to the job than watching the numbers. She watches the dust- and muck-encrusted underbellies for flashes of metal. ("If anything is shiny on an older truck, it's because a component is moving," she says. The shine is usually a sign of metal-on-metal abrasion that indicates broken or worn components.) She watches, as each truck slows, the outer workings of its braking system. ("If you sit a certain way, you can watch the push rods to see how far they're travelling. And if they're travelling too far we'll pull them around back and do a brake check.")

She watches for bald tires and flat tires, which can often go undetected by the driver, especially if the offending rubber is the innermost partner of a side-by-side pair. She checks for spent lights, loads fastened too loosely to flatbeds, fuel leaks, sagging suspensions, cracked windshields, malfunctioning wiper blades. She also checks for licence, registration, insurance, and, in a few keystrokes, the driver's safety record (and that of his company), and the driver's criminal record. She'll look, too, at the hours-of-service logbook and the trip-inspection report, not to mention the certificate of dangerous-goods handling if the circumstance demands.

Often she finds life-endangering deficiencies. She once examined a tanker hauling liquid hydrogen and found a cracked suspension spring. She put her finger on the breached metal and rubbed off the carbon residue. The metal-on-metal friction was causing a spark at every pothole.

"I showed it to the driver and the blood drained from his head," she says. "All's he had to hit was a big bump in the road and it would have been over. Boom! It would have been like a bomb in the middle of the highway. I think that was the highlight of my career."

Mike, who is working on a computer nearby, raises his head when Jax asks him for the highlight of his wreck-off-the-road career. He says the list is too long, but he has seen a suspension put together with a treated four-by-four so the truck wouldn't collapse. He has seen wheels held on without any nuts.

"For some guys, breaking the law is the cost of doing business," Mike says.

Says Jax: "These guys are under big time constraints. They've got a boss saying, 'Get out there, get that load delivered.' And some of them don't do their pre-trip inspections like they should, so they end up staying with us for the day until they get fixed."

Her sympathy only goes so far. Even when the Ministry of Transportation holds an announced safety blitz – meaning it makes truckers and truck companies aware of its plan to randomly pull over trucks during, say, a three-day window – it still finds about 19.5 per cent of the trucks aren't road-worthy and are put out of service until they're repaired. When the ministry holds unannounced blitzes, randomly pulling over trucks without warning, the out-of-service statistics surge to about 41.5 per cent.

Today there is no blitz, announced or not. Today Jax and her colleagues – who work in a brown brick building fitted with large windows of tinted glass – are simply pulling over trucks that either weigh too much or don't look right, or, for whatever reason, set off the inspector's internal alarm. This inspection station used to be open twenty-four hours a day, but staff cuts have limited the hours, which safety advocates say is unwise. A 2004 study paid for by the Michigan Truck Safety Commission concluded that increasing the number of inspections was an effective way to reduce the number of unsafe trucks on the road. The study found that for every 1,000 inspections of commercial vehicles, 0.86 lives are saved, 19.97 crashes are avoided, and 13.69 injuries are prevented. Ontario's Ministry of Transportation conducted 143,000 roadside inspections in 2004, which means enforcement officers can say with some measure of statistical certainty that they saved about 123 lives with the effort. But the union that represents enforcement officers has pointed out that Ontario hasn't replaced the seventy-some enforcement officials it has recently lost to attrition.

"The premier has a choice: Save money or save lives," says Joe Daniel, a union spokesman. "We are telling him to fill those positions now. It might not happen today and it might not happen tomorrow or even two years or three years from now, but without sufficient enforcement trucking safety is going to become a much bigger problem than it is right now, and by then it will be too late to fix the problem. We are raising a flag up right now before it's too late. As soon as trucking companies know the enforcement's not as strict as it once was, where do they look to save money? They look to save money on truck repairs. There are operators who'll take advantage of the situation knowing full well they don't have as many officers out there looking after them."

Jax, reclining by her computer screen, notes the numbers on a white truck painted with blue flames. It's 1,100 kilograms overweight. The driver gets the pull-over signal and dutifully guides his truck behind the inspection station. Jax walks out of the building to the holding area. The driver, a large man with a bushy, greying beard, rolls down his window and hands over his paperwork.

"My boss is a diesel mechanic so she should be in tip-top shape," he says from behind the wheel.

"Who?" says Jax. "Your boss?"

The big man laughs a tense laugh.

"I'm going to do a quick inspection, because it's not pretty."

As Jax makes her rounds of the rig – which is not pretty because it's covered in rust and caked in dirt – the driver steps out onto the tarmac. Darren, as it turns out, is wearing a T-shirt with the words "Doesn't Play Well With Others" and a belt, a ring, and a bracelet bearing the logo of the Harley-Davidson motorcycle company. His triceps, blue flames in ink, match his paint job. Jax is behind the trailer now, noting the decided lack of blue paint on the licence plate. The faded numbers are all but imperceptible from any distance.

"There's a ticket for that," she says, "but he seems like a really nice guy."

She boards a small dolly, the kind mechanics use to traverse the undersides of cars, and prepares to begin her sub-truck look-see. Before she does, she takes a deep breath and sucks in her stomach.

"This," she says, "is why you don't eat too many dough-nuts."

This, too, is why she's not wearing what is supposed to be standard equipment for her ilk: a bulletproof vest. Crawling around on pavement in the hazy heat makes a cotton shirt feel oppressive. Strapping Kevlar to one's core would seem to greatly increase one's chances of a trip to the hospital for a rendezvous with a dehydration-induced IV. Jax is well aware of an estimate that's made the rounds – that some 80 per cent of drivers pack guns. She'll deflect bullets with her charm.

"If I wore the vest, I'd faint," she says. "But don't tell my boss."

She's examining the belly now, slowly rolling from

front to back while checking for loose components, suspicious rattles, leaks, and cracks and whatever else doesn't look right.

"Basically you start putting your hands on everything," she says.

Darren has his hands nervously grasped in front of his belly. Today he's hauling a trailer-load of bushings around the Greater Toronto Area. It's a good job, he says, even if he puts in twelve-hour days for about $250. Years ago he travelled wider and made less.

"I used to haul automotive freight, so I made out not too bad," he said. "I owned my own truck, and after insurance and the price of fuel – well, it killed you. But I was just on the road too long, and it was time to stay home with the family."

Jax is mid-trailer now, taking a second look at what looks like a wonky brake setup. She asks Darren to get back in the truck and push the pedal, then shakes her head.

"Neither one of the push rods is moving," she says, reemerging from below.

Darren raises his bushy eyebrows above the rims of his dark sunglasses.

"Everybody has these notions that big bearded dudes are evil and terrible," Jax says to me. "But they're average guys, most of them. Now, I wouldn't want to hang out with them in their spare time – who knows at that point?"

She has endured more intimate relations with a less desirable population. For four years she was a guard at a women's prison. She has a fingernail-wide scar on the knuckle of her left thumb as a conversation piece that proves it. She got the scar in a prison riot, the work of a sharpened toothbrush fitted with the nasty bit of a disposable razor. The makeshift shiv was wielded by a prisoner offended by Jax's handling of a significant other.

"She was mad because I was holding her girlfriend against the wall. Nasty girls," she says. "I put my hand up to block [the toothbrush-razor] because I knew it was coming for my face. So it could have been worse. But it dug right into the bone. It wasn't fun."

Darren, unsolicited, tells the story of a friend, a member of the Hells Angels, who died recently in a motorcycle accident. A tractor-trailer making a turn didn't see him. He was killed instantly.

"That's my biggest fear, killing somebody," Darren says, his voice trailing off.

Back to the inspection, Jax has Darren turn on his ignition, which in turn pressurizes the braking system, which allows Darren to demonstrate that the push rods that were thought to be faulty were in fact only stuck. They're moving acceptably now, and Jax is moving on, finishing up her once-over and rubbing pebbles from her hands. At this point she's faced with an option, she says. She can go by the book and write Darren a ticket for each of his violations, for the balding tire and the illegible plate and even, if she felt mean, for the brakes that didn't respond on the first try. But she's not going to go by the book.

"This is my way of thinking: If I had found a bunch of stuff, I might have started writing tickets," she says. "Four out of five guys back here (in the inspection station) would have given him a ticket, but I don't want to kill a guy's month. The truck was basically in good order. There were a couple of small things."

Darren is back in his cab, his old engine idling. There will be no tickets, but there will also be no sticker for his windshield that allows other enforcement officers to identify trucks that have been recently inspected. To get the sticker, he'll have to return with a replaced tire. He says he will. Jax waves him off, and the truck rumbles and bobs as it rejoins the road.

"It's probably one of the only jobs where you can see you've made a difference right away," she says. "Because if a truck comes in with bad brakes, the potential that you saved somebody's life – no one died because of that truck – there's that instant gratification knowing you've saved somebody's life. I think only a surgeon can say that.

"We had some trucks fixed today that had the potential to harm somebody. This job, every day I go home, at least one of us has saved lives today. No doubt."

5

Method in the Bottle, Swamp Doggies, and the Rockies

I t's a pristine August evening. The cicadas are humming, the humidity is weighing, and I am driving with my wife, Andrea, to Toronto's industrial outskirts, where I'm to meet up with two truckers from the Calgary area who will be bound for Vancouver in a matter of a couple of hours. We are pulling closer to the Mississauga base of Reimer Transport, the sun is low in the sky, and I am explaining to Andrea how it is possible that in fifty-some hours, I plan to be stretching my legs with a walk along the Stanley Park seawall. Between here and there, my wheel-manning companions and I will traverse more than two-thirds of Canada's East-West span in a shade over two days, stopping only for driver changes and quick meals.

"They don't really stop for much," I say, explaining the modus operandi of the driver team, which is to keep the truck moving to maximize profit.

"Not even to shower?" Andrea says.

"Not even to pee," I say.

I am exaggerating for effect. I can provide an alibi for hundreds of truckers, beside whom I've stood facing respectable evacuation facilities from the Subarctic to the Atlantic Coast. But I have also been to the Fergus Truck Show in Ontario, where I distinctly remember disposing of a coffee cup, only to be startled by a peek at the trash can's contents. Atop the waste was a large box of mineral water, a dozen bottles neatly arranged inside, four by three. But the bottles were neither empty nor filled with water. They were filled to various depths with a yellowy substance – too Day-Glo to be apple juice; too unappealing to be a sports drink – that I could only assume was urine. I knew I wasn't mistaken. So widespread is the trucker's habit of finding relief in a bottle that at least one U.S. state, Oregon, has actually passed a law that prohibits the roadside disposal of urine-filled containers. The passing of the law was prompted by the complaints of highway maintenance crews who'd been frequently splattered with the caustic liquid when their mower blades met the offensive litter.

The state of Washington even launched a truck-stop poster campaign that centred around a picture of a plastic milk jug filled with an unmistakable yellow liquid. The caption read: "Okay, one last time: This is not a urinal." The fine print threatened: "Get caught tossing a bottle of urine and you'll pay $95." According to an official with Washington State's Department of Ecology, one road crew found 2,666 bottles of urine in a year.

I share these facts with Andrea, no fan of bathroom humour, and she says, "You're getting your own bottle."

I say, "Don't worry about that."

She says, "You're not peeing into someone else's bottle." And so she compels me to stop at a fuelling station, where I buy a large cylinder of mineral water while I observe the truckers at a tucked-away table, three men in turbans gazing blankly into steaming cups.

I arrive at the appointed yard and bid Andrea adieu.

"I'll wait for a few minutes, just to make sure," she says.

And sure enough, after I'm told the Vancouver-bound departure time has been pushed back a couple of hours, I am jogging back to the car and headed for a late dinner to kill the delay.

Take two – a 10:30 p.m. return to the Reimer head-quarters – goes better. I'm immediately shown to a basement room where two dispatchers, Steve and Don, are calling the hotel rooms of their long-haul employees, rousing them for their evening departures.

"Room 311, please," Steve says into the phone. "Unit 704? Hi, it's Steve over at Reimer. Your truck will be ready soon. Great. See you in a bit."

My drivers, Rey and Jeff, are just arriving from their hotel, where they'd pulled in during the wee hours of the morning and had been sleeping most of the day. Before I meet them, I'm introduced to a handful of Reimer's union-ized city drivers, men whose travels never take them farther than a five-hundred-mile radius from Toronto. The Team-sters, a half-dozen of them, are standing in the parking lot, their truck routes long done for the day, waiting for their 3-to-11 shift to be over.

We exchange pleasantries, we talk sports, and soon they're razzing me about my pending journey.

"By the time you get to Regina, you'll be drinking," says a man in a Toronto Maple Leafs cap. "By the time you get to Calgary, you'll be doing dope."

Don, who had just called me a poor bastard, says, "This business sucks. I wouldn't take the trip you're taking for ten thousand bucks."

On that note, I say goodbye to the city drivers and, seeing a green Peterbilt pulling up to the scale a short hike across the yard, I walk over and meet my soon-to-be hosts. Jeff, whom I'd said hello to inside, shakes my hand again and introduces me to Rey. Rey is wearing dark blue Wrangler jeans and black leather shoes with fringed ornamentation from the laces toward the toes. The shoes recall golf spikes from an earlier era. Rey looks a bit like Dan Reeves, the football coach, only with longer hair that curls at the back and the top and is cut into an extreme part on the right side. Rey owns the truck; Jeff is his friend and employee (although Rey refers to Jeff more than once as his partner). For a moment we stand under the glow of the yard's harsh lamps. Then Rey and Jeff resume their pre-trip preparations. Jeff is concluding the most recent update of his logbook: "Amazing things the government makes us do," he says, closing his book. "Well, we got that beat. I guess we can take off, eh?"

Rey, meanwhile, is checking the tires with a hammer, standard procedure to ensure there isn't a flat hidden among the rows of rubber. The green Peterbilt, a square-nosed classic from the 2002 model year, appears as aerodynamic as a stack of concrete blocks. Indeed, while more than a couple of manufacturers have streamlined their designs to improve fuel efficiency, this traditional model's chunky profile hasn't changed much since the 1970s. There are chrome fuel tanks, chrome wheel caps, chrome exhaust stacks, all nods to another era. But inside there are no old-days hardships.

"This truck drives like a sports car," says Jeff. "Mind you, not many sports cars weigh 81,000 pounds."

Indeed, with a fifty-three-foot trailer full of cargo, the rig is grossing 81,895 pounds. I ask what's in the load, but Rey and Jeff don't know, and they can't open the sealed trailer to take a look. It's not that the seal is impenetrable; it is merely a piece of aluminum, a little wider and sturdier than a garbage-bag twist tie, etched with a number that corresponds to their paperwork.

"It's lots of little loads," says Jeff. "All we know is there's some dangerous goods. They've got to tell us about that. But everything else, we don't get the benefit of that knowledge. And that's fine with us."

The drivers' ignorance of their cargo is to their liking for a couple of reasons. For one, it tends to absolve them as suspects if their load happens to fall victim to thieves. (Trailer theft is a $1-billion annual problem for Canada's trucking business, and it's more rampant in the United States, where its prevalence adds an estimated one hundred dollars to the price of every personal computer, according to one insurer.) For another, it means they don't actually have to unload it. The vast majority of non-unionized truckers aren't anywhere near as lucky. They spend much-lamented time and energy schlepping their cargo from trailer to loading dock. Most of the work is unpaid and not logged, or it is paid in a flat fee no matter how long it takes. It's been estimated that North American drivers spend as much as thirty to forty hours a week either waiting to unload or unloading their trailers, which means they put in what many people consider a full week, standing around or carrying boxes, and then, when their truck is rolling, they begin to get paid by the mile.

Jeff and Rey, though, members of the Canadian Auto Workers union, will simply drive this shipment to the Reimer yard in suburban Vancouver, then head to a complimentary hotel to sleep in preparation for their return leg. The loading, the unloading – it's all somebody else's worry, which makes the work all the more enviable. They do know that this trip is requiring them to display a diamond-shaped placard bearing the number eight on both sides and both ends of the trailer. The placards are known as safety marks. The number eight means it's a Class 8 dangerous good, a corrosive. There are nine classes, which are broken down into an extensive list of sub-classes. Class 1 is explosives, Class 2 gases, Class 3 flammable liquids, and Class 4 flammable solids, spontaneous combustibles, and substances that, on contact with water, emit flammable gases. To see a Class 4 safety mark at the scene of an accident would be helpful information for firefighters rushing bearing hoses.

The moon is nearly full. Jeff stokes the engine and we start out through the puddled tarmac of Toronto's outskirts, past faded signs in pot-holed parking lots, heading briefly west then abruptly north.

"It's a nice drive through Ontario," says Jeff. "We've got moose up in Northern Ontario to contend with tonight. I saw a half a dozen on the way down, just on one shift."

Talk of moose reminded me of an afternoon I spent on the fringes of St. John's, Newfoundland, where the fog was lying low and the truck stop was slick with mist, and the truckers, standing at fuelling islands with their hoods up and their shoulders hunched, told tales of near misses. Out east it's common to see trucks outfitted with hulking aluminum grills known affectionately as moose catchers. The grills look like horizontal jail-cell bars. They're designed so that if the worst-case scenario happens and a 1,400-pound prince of the Canadian bog comes between them and the destination, the truck will deliver more punishment than it takes. Moose are hard animals for motorists and truckers to avoid, especially at night. Their hair, dull brown, isn't especially reflective, even with today's high-powered halogen headlights. Their dark eyes don't sparkle like bike pedals in the glare. They are attracted to the roadside mostly in the spring, when the thaw brings cool water seasoned with road salt. And unlike most animals, their fight-or-flight mechanism leans heavily away from flight. They'll stand their ground and, more than likely, die. But they might not go to waste. To dispose of traffic kills, some states have roadkill lists. State troopers, when they become aware of a vehicle-animal collision, arrive on the scene and, if necessary, put the mammal out of its misery. Then they call the first person on the roadkill list, who has the right of first refusal on salvaging the meat.

Technology is helping stem the carnage. Some jurisdictions employ signs equipped with motion detectors that trip a flashing light that warns approaching vehicles of an animal's presence in the road. Mirrors on the shoulder can reflect oncoming headlights toward the side of the road and, in doing so, frighten animals back into the safety of the dark bushes. Whistles mounted on bumpers and grills emit a high-frequency squeal that manufacturers claim inspires everything from deer to elk to possums to take heed and clear the area.

Back on the Trans-Canada, Jeff gives me a quick course in our trip's other details. We could get to Vancouver faster than the scheduled ETA, he says, but fuel economy, not raw speed, is the goal. He and Rey believe they've found the truck's efficiency "sweet spot."

"The faster you go, the more air you're pushing," he says, "and the more fuel you're burning."

Both Jeff and Rey grew up on farms around Verdun, Manitoba. Jeff's father was a farmer and so, for a while, was Jeff. The family raised pigs on about thirty acres of land a few hours west of Winnipeg.

"I didn't like pig farming one bit, not one bit," he says. "In high school I went framing houses, working construction. But ever since I was a young little jerk I wanted to be a truck driver. It was the travel. I thought it'd be the greatest job in the world. And I still don't mind this line of work.

"But there's no honour any more. Now everybody gets mad at each other. I remember stopping by the side of the road and two or three trucks would stop and make sure you were all right, to see if you were broken down and needed help. Now . . ."

When Jeff began his trucking career in the late 1970s, technology wasn't spoiling its benefactors. He drove a 1974 cabover Ford, a reliable enough machine until the wind blew and the snow fell and the temperatures dropped. In those conditions the truck's internal parts – most notably the driver – had a tendency to freeze. Jeff wore a snowmobile suit and thick gloves when he drove that Ford. A heater existed, in theory, but it was basically useless in seasons not named spring and autumn. And so one sub-zero night, when the contents of his fuel filter turned from slush to ice and he was stopped on the roadside on the outskirts of some prairie outpost, he worried for a moment that he'd be spending an uncomfortably cold evening at the roadside. But within moments, three fellow truckers had pulled over to help, one of whom happened to have the necessary part in his toolbox.

"He didn't even charge me for the filter," says Jeff. "He said, 'Next time.' Nowadays you wouldn't see that. Nowadays a guy sees you're stranded, he'd charge you triple."

As he speaks, Jeff is pulling into the parking lot of our first stop, the Esso at Nairn Centre, where we arrive for a driver switch and a bathroom break. When last we were walking in the summer sweetness – in that suburban

Toronto parking lot – the air was heavy like hot breath, soupy and hard to breathe. But here it's crisp and chilled. Inhalation is a pleasure. As we step into the door of the small store, we are greeted by a wall of stuffed Canadiana, plush bears and moose and beavers. But there is no time for souvenir searching; in less than four minutes Jeff and Rey have returned to the truck, Rey setting down his coffee on the floor as he puts the machine in gear and rolls west. We are but one five-hour shift into the proceedings and already I'm flagging, my eyelids drooping, my will weakening. At this moment it does not surprise me that a U.S. Department of Transportation survey once included the revelation that 28 per cent of drivers reported falling asleep at the wheel at least once in the preceding month. Riding in a rig, for me and apparently for others, can be hypnotic, trance-inducing, sleep-bringing.

I drift off and jolt awake, not wanting Rey to witness my lack of stamina. But soon he's suggesting I climb to the top bunk, offering me earplugs for my snooze, the same kind he wears when he needs sleep. I feel groggy beyond disturbance. I turn down the plugs and hop into the top bunk, covering myself with the thin blue bedsheet I've brought along.

My head hits the pillow – make that the rolled-up T-shirt I have fashioned into a pillow – and I am asleep.

Sleeping in a truck's bunk is like sleeping in an earthquake. You shake. It's like you're hooked up to a vibrating strap, the kind once thought to speed weight loss. You bounce from side to side, hugging the back wall of the bunk one minute, threatening to fall over the forward edge the next. But because you've been looking at a white line for hours, because your body is glad for the chance to stretch itself after prolonged sitting, you sleep – albeit with the frequent interruptions supplied by potholes and lane changes and rumble-strip transgressions.

It is hardly as peaceful as lying down in the sleeper berth of a night train that gently rocks its passengers to sleep with the calming clunk-clunk of its progress. But as much as some would like to romanticize the beauty of riding the rails – as much as some would like to go back to a day when this continent's citizens and cargo moved by train – there is no going back. The day of the railroad's demise, or at the least a portent to its doom, has been traced to the 1867 Paris Exposition, which saw the introduction of the bicycle. The two-wheeled wonder proffered freedom from the schedule and the rail. It promised a kind of go-one's-own-way independence that was achievable only on horseback or foot. But pleasurable cycling required decent roads. And while France and other European countries had long invested in those – Napoleon would build a network of highways thanks to the good students of his country's School of Bridges and Roads, which was founded in 1747 – North American roads were abysmal. Farmers had, in some areas, a few months of the year when they could haul their produce in wagons without bogging down in mud on the dirt tracks that passed for thoroughfares.

America's railways had their limits, as was demonstrated when they failed miserably at meeting the demand to transport the 2 million American troops to the seaports where they'd set sail for the First World War. It didn't help that railway barons – men rich beyond the wildest dreams of even enterprising types – built up decades of ill will with a public that gawked at their luxurious lifestyles in the dime magazines of the day. Profits were high. Service wasn't great. And the backlash was inevitable after William Vanderbilt, when asked by the Chicago *Daily News* if his railroad would suffer a loss if the public interest was served, famously intoned, "The public be damned!"

It was in Woodrow Wilson's 1916 re-election campaign that he spoke the words: "It is perfectly obvious that you have got to have an intricate and perfect network of roads throughout the length and breadth of this great continent before you will have released the energies of America." The campaign for good roads soon took hold. As Stephen B. Goddard pointed out in his 1994 book *Getting There: The Epic Struggle Between Road and Rail in the American Century*, while railroads were a fortune builder for the already rich, trucks were an entrepreneurial opportunity for the everyman. "The Average Joe might become a wage slave for a railroad, but for just a few hundred dollars down payment, he could buy a truck for $2,000 to $5,000, take eighteen months to pay, and become captain of his fate. By the late 1920s – the heyday of the independent trucker – two-thirds of the three million trucks on American roads were operator owned. Those who owned most of the rest had five trucks or fewer. For millions, it was the American dream come true."

Many new truckers knew little about business and so they often went bust, a phenomenon that was repeated post-deregulation, when so many small players, eager to undercut the big companies but unschooled in the intricacies of running their small business on wheels, saw their dream towed away by the repo man. But trucking, both in the 1920s and 1930s – and, to be sure, in the deregulated era of the 1980s and 1990s – grew "like a field of weeds," writes Goddard, because of the low cost of entry into the business and the relatively small amount of know-how required; because railroads couldn't supply the demand for the movement of goods; and because trucks, not confined to rails, were infinitely more flexible. Thomas MacDonald, of the U.S. Federal Bureau of Roads, once claimed that America's Civil War could have been avoided had his country enjoyed the benefit of an interstate highway system in the 1860s, had southerners been able to visit Maine on holiday and northerners venture south for golf.

Perhaps owing to its indisputable role in nation-building, Canada's railway business has been heavily subsidized in Canada; from 1927 to 1991 it received $11 billion in government help, which dwarfs the $870 million that was paid to trucking companies during the same period. But the rails, while they have found their niche in the post-NAFTA economy, don't appear poised to topple trucking's dominance. In 2000, 23 per cent of Canadian exports to the United States, mostly raw materials, went by train. Just 9 per cent of U.S. exports to Canada could say the same. But railway advocates point to the damaging toll trucks

take on roads and the environment and argue that trucking interests are, indeed, subsidized by the government's
commitment to maintaining road infrastructure. Inter-
modal transportation – which is centred around the usage
of a standard container that universally fits on cargo ships,
trains, and properly fitted semi-trailers – can compete
with trucking when the distances are longer, beyond eight
hundred to sixteen hundred kilometres. But it still makes
up a small portion of the transport business. Trucking
still dominates.

Just as quickly as I'd fallen asleep, I'm awake. I am
awake so soon because Rey has pulled the truck over and
he and Jeff are fumbling to attach the black strap that
hangs from the bottom of my bunk to the truck's header.
It's a safety device meant to ensure that, in the event of a
sudden halt to the B.C.-bound travel, the occupant of the
top bunk doesn't cross the Manitoba border while the
bunk is in Ontario. But for all their handyman wiles,
neither trucker can figure out how the strap attaches. I
pretend I'm sleeping and I hear them fussing: "Push down
. . . Lift up . . . No, not like that . . . It goes like this . . ." But
they soon quit trying and I'm soon sleeping, albeit without
a safety strap.

When I awake, it's 8:06 a.m.; my nap has lasted about
four hours. I stumble into the passenger seat, squinting.
The radio is telling me what the horizon already knows:
the forecast is for shine all over the province. The reflection
off the chrome is blinding. We roll past a sign for the
Algoma Rod and Gun Club, past an electric billboard

flashing the phrase STAY ALERT, STAY ALIVE. We're a couple of hours out of Wawa, driving north on Lake Superior's eastern shore, and Rey is speaking of the decade he spent running solo on a California produce run.

"Hectic, hectic pace," he says. "When you closed the doors on the trailer, it was always a day late. They always wanted it yesterday or the day before was even better. This is a lot more laid back, two guys running team. We're never in a real hurry to get there."

We roll through cut-outs of the Canadian Shield, over sloes, past barns, by old inns and rolling hills and leaning birches. We are on Highway 17 North, running past shimmering lakes backed by verdant hills, and Rey is marvelling at the landscape as enthusiastically as I am, telling his story as we breeze west. He knew he wanted to be a truck driver at age seven, when one of his older brothers took him on a big-rig road trip and he fell in love with the machinery and the motion. He drove a pickup truck on country roads at age nine. "I probably had to stand up to reach the pedals," he remembers. He drove feed trucks and lumber trucks and flatbed trailers topped with farm machines from Winnipeg to Calgary and Edmonton.

"My wife, she pretty much raised the kids herself," he says. "Had I been doing this then, team driving for Reimer, it would have been better. You sometimes look back and wish you'd made different choices."

We're in Wawa for an early lunch, but we don't see the goose, the famous sheet-metal sculpture of the great Canadian migrator. We see the tiny, not-so-clean bathroom at the Family Kitchen Restaurant. One toilet, one urinal, one sink, no paper towels, no soap. It is not exactly a full-service truck stop, but it's a typical haunt of my companions.

The booths are fake-look wood with seats of rusty vinyl. The ceiling is yellow. The tables have white plastic tops set with paper placemats that greet you with a message. They say, "Season's Greetings."

Jeff sits down and begins to remove a sliver from his right middle finger with a pocket knife. When he's finished he picks up his placemat, turns it over, and sighs: "No games on the other side? No mazes?"

Says Rey, in mock outrage: "Nothing to colour?"

"Tough day."

The waitress cocks her head and laughs. It's a Tuesday. Jeff and Rey were here last on Sunday, dining on their east-bound journey.

Rey is wearing a black leather vest over a black shirt trimmed with a print of rodeo cowboys riding bulls. Jeff is wearing a polo shirt with four buttons, one of which is fastened, and a black leather ball cap with the words "Peterbilt Winnipeg" embroidered on the face. Their necks are hung with gold chains.

I'm tired, as always, so I order coffee. Jeff, who will soon be manning the throttle, joins me. Rey, because he is due for his shift in the bunk, sticks to water. We order food — eggs and bacon for Jeff and me, a toasted Western for Rey — and we're back in the truck in twenty minutes.

"Well, we'll catch you later," Rey says, zipping the curtain closed.

"Yeah, have a pleasant nap," says Jeff. And we're off, past campgrounds and Catfish Lake and the Lakewood Motel, into a sunny mid-morning. I am noticing that the controls in Rey's truck are elaborate. The dashboard is fashioned of a convincing rosewood-esque plastic and all the gauges – and the switches, labelled in ornate script, for the Engine Brake and Fifth Wheel and so on – are trimmed with chrome. They're expensive upgrades, some of which have been made by Jeff, though he owns no portion of the truck, in a gesture of goodwill.

"It makes it more unique from the other guys," says Jeff, looking out the windshield past another nod to customization, a pair of cowboy-hat air fresheners hanging from the bracket that suspends the CB above the windshield.

We're still on 17 North, doing a steady 90 km/h. In the scrub east of Thunder Bay, Jeff takes a small black case from above the dash, opens the zipper, and clears his throat.

"You like Elton John?" he says.

"Who doesn't?" I say.

We are nearing Marathon, Ontario. Rain is starting to pelt the windshield. Jeff flips on the wipers and cranks Sir Elton.

"Without love," sings Elton. "I believe in love."

In a moment, we see police lights. An officer of the provincial police, sheltered by an orange slicker and a wide-brim hat, is halting traffic around a tricky curve.

"He must like a wet seat," says Jeff. The cop's driver-side door is open to the drizzle.

The delay, we find out, has been caused by the retrieval of lumber that had fallen off a flatbed as it rounded the bend.

After a ten-minute pause, we're allowed to pass as young men in ball caps emerge from the ditch with cracked slabs of particle board in their hands. And so we resume our regular cruising speed, passing Schreiber, home of Dominic Fillaine (Canadian Boxing Champion 1990, 1992), passing forested hills draped in roiling clouds, passing the islands of Lake Superior. In some places the road is but a short step from the shore of the greatest of lakes.

We're up a hill at 45 km/h, streams of cars and mini-vans and pickup trucks whizzing past us. The slow pace, though, is out of our control; we're behind a flatbed loaded with lumber (this load apparently tightly secured). We follow our pacesetter through swirling fog, to the hill's crest, then down again to the big lake, to a moving vista.

"Perdy scenery," says Jeff. "Now, that's the sort of thing people sitting in an office all day don't get to see – except when they're on vacation, of course."

What the office workers aren't seeing is a stand of birches, some silver, some white, framing the big lake's rippling waters, the shadows of faraway hills, a fifty-fifty sky, part violence, part bliss, the bleached-white bursts of puffy clouds, the sad-grey veins of storm bringers.

We're about an hour outside of Thunder Bay. It's sunny for a moment, and Jeff says, "It looks like it's clearing up." But the westerly wind soon pushes fog in our face. We make a quick stop in the gloom of Pass Lake, a driver switch, and three phone calls home, and Rey is pointing the Peterbilt toward Thunder Bay. The road is like a conveyor belt into some haunted house, the fog soupy and spooky. We pass a kid on a bike riding westbound on the eastbound shoulder. In the rare glimpses of horizon, I'm looking for the Sleeping Giant – the rock formation that resembles a very large man lying prone that is Thunder Bay's backdrop – but it is hidden under the low blanket.

We turn onto the 102 West, and as we pass the inspection station, Rey jumps in his seat.

"Oh my goodness that scale is never open," he says. "But the gate is open, there's a car in there, and I didn't see if those lights were flashing. Oh well, if they request my presence, they'll catch up with me."

No one gives chase, but soon Rey is slowing down all the same. Two dogs, one black, one white, are haughtily occupying the westbound lane, running dangerous zigzags as we approach. For a minute they abandon the road and Rey feathers the throttle as though he's ready to get back to speed. But the mutts cross our path again, and then, in the middle of the road, they stop. And then we're right on top of them. Rey can't see either dog in front of his nose. He can only see two kids on bikes at the roadside, both of them looking horrified.

Rey sounds panicked, knowing that if he'd hit the dogs, their demises might not register: "Where's he at? Where are they at?"

I finally spotted the dogs on the shoulder. Crisis averted.

"That doesn't happen very often," says Rey. "Not too traffic-wise."

We turn back onto 11-17 West. The stormy purple sky is throwing noisy droplets of cold water on the windshield. We pass a sign: "Beware of Moose at Night." Now it's pouring, 6:30 p.m., and we see a female moose enjoying a salty drink in the eastbound ditch.

Rey turns to address the dashboard. It's vibrating.

"I have to dig into that," he says. "I'll have to take the glove compartment off and get behind there and tighten something. It sure is annoying."

In December of 1994, Rey decided he'd had enough of hauling produce. His brother had been working for Reimer for a couple of years, "ranting and raving" about how good the company was. But Rey was skeptical about sharing his ride with a partner.

"It was always something I looked at sort of disdainfully," he says. "I said I'd never do it. It's a challenge. Being able to get along with each other, the truck is close confines. It's not an easy thing to find two guys who can see semi-sort-of eye-to-eye."

There's a semi-sort-of pause as Rey gives a passing truck the big-shooter finger.

"It has its challenges, its ups and downs, good days and bad days. But nothing you can't overcome," he says. "I think I probably was surprised. If somebody had told me we'd still be doing this eight and a half years later, I would have said, 'I don't think so.' It's been a good haul. If I was to go out and find somebody else, I'd have to work hard at it.

"There always seems to be people who can't put up with each other or don't get along. A lot of guys push it to the limit to try to beat the system – I know I did. The team setup does allow you more time at home. I know I've changed my whole mindset from years ago. I know I used to be a whole lot more aggressive myself."

Tempering his aggressiveness has been economical.

"I started to realize going 55 or 60 instead of 70 or 75, I was seeing a lot more of this [he rubbed his finger and thumb together to signify cash]. That was just going out of the stack when I was speeding. Costs are high and there's only a few things you have control over. Our rates are set so you've got to control your costs where you can."

As we keep rolling over the Northern Ontario rocklands, we pass an eastbound train stacked double-high with containers. There's a sign on the right shoulder: "Moose on the Loose." And, approaching in the eastbound lanes, a truck marked with the logo of TransX, a name that draws a chuckle from Rey.

"They employ what we like to call new Canadians," he says. "I don't understand them. I can't get my head around it. I mean, not to paint them all with the same brush, but I've had some very close calls with them, and they've been very aggressive. Like, I mean, passing on an uphill, around a curve, double yellow line. Like, how did he know nobody else was coming?"

The TransX rig didn't get the benefit of Rey's big-shooter gesture. A few moments later, he offered his trademark acknowledgement to an armoured car, then declined to raise the digit to a large civilian van. We pass through Atikokan, Canoe Capital of Canada, and by the time we're sixty kilometres from Dryden, we're trading glances with a driver from the Mill Creek Trucking Company. Rey tells the story of how, a couple of years back, a Reimer truck and a Mill Creek truck hit head-on, killing all four drivers. The Mill Creek truck was occupied by a husband-wife team. Rey knew both of the Reimer drivers.

"A lot of times what happens is a husband and wife will drive team, the wife will get her licence, but she's a little inexperienced, so the husband will end up doing most of the driving," Rey says. "So he ends up being way too tired, driving past his limit, using her logbook to make it look like a legal situation. What can you do?

"There were lots of times when I shouldn't have been out there, either. But I never had a mishap, whatever that's worth."

I see a dead moose at the roadside. I see a beaver dam. And then I see white crosses staked on the eastbound shoulder, the site of the crash. As we pass the humble memorial, in the orange glow of August dusk, Rey gives the big-shooter finger to no truck in particular.

At Dryden, we halt for grub. Rey and I order chicken clubs. Jeff goes with the hamburger steak, a dish whose moniker initially confuses an outsider.

I say, "What's a hamburger steak?"

Jeff says, "It's a hamburger without the bun."

This meal does not keep us long, and we're back in gear within a half-hour.

"I used to listen to a lot of audio books," Jeff says when I ask him how he manages to keep his sanity. "Oh man, that passes the time. But eventually, you get to the point where you've heard 'em all. Elmore Leonard, John le Carré, Mary Higgins Clark, even some Danielle Steel, although that was very rare. I even did some Stephen King – that kept me awake at night. Those stories have a way of keeping a guy awake at night."

We pass some more signs: "Be Aware of Moose at Night," warns one. "Fatigue Kills. Take a Break," insists another.

But Jeff is nursing coffee, looking for moose – he calls them swamp doggies – and pondering the chemistry of his partnership.

"I never was very keen on the idea," he says. "It's awfully hard to find someone you can get along with. Plus, it's hard to find someone you can trust. One guy I used to drive with, he scared the crap out of me. I'd be lying in the back, and he'd be running onto those rumble strips. If I had to run team with somebody I didn't trust, I wouldn't do it . . . Rey, he's a very good driver. I know he can climb back there when I'm driving so he must have some confidence in my ability also."

Jeff remembers a moment that defines their mutual trust. It was winter in Chicago a couple of years back. The roads were slick with sleet. Jeff, lying in the bottom bunk, knew something was wrong because he heard the wheels spinning. For a moment, he was nervous enough to consider popping his head into the cab.

"But Rey was driving," he says, "so I just turned over and went to sleep."

We drive on into the purple bruise of darkness. Our windshield hits a firefly. Its luminescence fades slowly in death. But there is another light show in our view in minutes. We're crossing the longitudinal centre of Canada when aurora borealis treats us to its ever-morphing charms. It's one of this planet's most amazing natural phenomena, to be sure, and I can only imagine my reaction to its visual impact if I hadn't been raised on biannual fireworks and laser shows and image projectors. I'm looking at the northern lights and then I'm sleeping. I'm looking, dozing, writing, dozing, commenting on my awe, and flat-out sleeping. So I hop into the bunk and make it official.

I awake, after a solid three hours, to another blue morning, to a grain elevator on my right, to Rey at the wheel saying, "It's going to be hot. They're saying southern Alberta, thirty-five Celsius." I'm seeing cattle grazing, black sloes at the roadside, Rey giving his finger to a Mill Creek driver, a sign that tells me we're just down the road from Melville, Saskatchewan, and 124 kilometres from Regina. And I'm hearing a CBC report on the radio that the CPR is cutting five hundred jobs.

We stop for coffee at the Great Plains Truck Stop in White City, Saskatchewan. I buy a paper and in doing so immediately provoke in-cab outrage. Jeff seethes at the front-page headline: Canada to Legalize Gay Marriage.

"Courts make the laws in this country," he says. "Bullshit. What are we paying our legislators for?"

The right lane is closed outside of Regina. The standstill prompts the black Dodge pickup truck we're trailing to pull off the road, navigate a dry ditch, and resume its westbound push on the parallel service road. Soon, there's a procession of pickup trucks following the black Dodge.

The prairies are the picture, and there's nothing much in the frame. There's grey pavement, the power lines standing at skewed attention, the rail line cutting through green and beige fields.

"It's a different kind of country entirely – peaceful in its own way," Jeff says. "Wintertime, it's rather drab-looking."

On this stretch of the Trans-Canada, you can't see the eastbound lane. It's hidden behind the rolling hill, which is exactly where it would be if you were designing the corridor with safety in mind. The fence beside the road consists of well-spread posts supporting four perpetual strands of barbed wire.

"I really like my country, wouldn't want to live anywhere else, but when it comes right down to it, the scenery's damn near the same in the United States. And they've generally got better roads than we have here," Jeff says. U.S. interstate highways are almost universally superior to Canada's coast-to-coast ribbon. They generally have wider shoulders, more gaping medians, longer merging lanes, gentler on- and off-ramps and smoother surfaces. "It's a darn good country we live in, though. I really like it. We just need to get someone from out west to be PM for a change. I'm a typical Westerner. It seems to me the people we have in Ottawa don't give a rat's ass about the west. The gun registry – it's not enforceable. It's not going to save any lives. Passing a law that's not enforceable is a whole shitload waste of money."

As he speaks we are literally bouncing down the pan-national highway.

"They vote NDP in this province. I think that's why their roads are so bad," Jeff says. "I lived in Manitoba for a lot of years with the NDP in power, and it seemed like whatever they touched turned to red ink."

Jeff lives in Okotoks, Alberta, a bedroom community of about twelve thousand about a half-hour southwest of Calgary. He's married to Kathy, and they have two cats and two dogs. One's a Pomeranian named Teiken, one's a Canaan – a German shepherd crossed with a greyhound, apparently – named Negev.

The roots of Jeff's trucking career are planted in a motorcycle tread. He bought said two-wheeler in high school. He had to make payments, so he finished Grade 11 and he hit the road. At the time he didn't miss classes, especially French.

"I refused to learn that language. Me and my friends, we were competing for the worst marks in class," he says. "I regret that now. I think it's a good thing to be multilingual. But there's a few things I regret. Shoulda saved some money instead of blowing it, maybe stayed in school a few more years. These days without a college education you can't get anywhere.

"There's no glamour in this. It's a tough slog. You see a lot of country. You see a lot of stuff. But I would rather be home with my feet up at night. If I could find a job that paid as well at home, I'd take it. It's a lifestyle. There's no romance or glamour to it. There's a lot of people who'd like to get into it or think it'd be neat. It's not what it appears to be. You're really making a big sacrifice. You don't have any social life. It's really hard to maintain friends. You get home, and all you've got time for is mowing the lawn, paying the bills."

Jeff estimates 80 per cent of truckers own guns. He has his arsenal, but they're all at home.

"What are you gonna do? Shoot someone?" he says. "Maybe the guy deserved it, maybe he didn't."

Gun or none, he has never liked travelling into U.S. urban centres. He has turned down every New York–bound shipment he has ever been offered. Once, when he made a rare trip to Los Angeles, a man hopped to his window wielding a gun, demanding two hundred dollars. He wanted the money for the gun, not from Jeff.

"I thought he was going to use the gun to rob me. When he showed it to me, I knew for darn sure it was a government Colt, a .45 Colt. They're keepsakes. I kinda wish I woulda bought it. It'd be worth $1,200 in Canada now."

The morning zings by. We're in Swift Current around noon local time. A truck passes on the left doing perhaps 130 km/h.

"Hammer down there, Bud," says Jeff. "You've got miles to make. That guy's from North Dakota. I'm very observant when it comes to licence plates. I don't miss many. It's something to pass the time with."

The rolling hills are suddenly populated by windmills, wind turbines. There are dinosaur fossils in these parts and to our right, the Trans-Canada is in the early stages of being twinned. The road-to-be is dirt now, but it's flat, ready for gravel and pavement.

"Should be done by winter. It'll be good for the people who follow us – they can pass us, and we can pass the tourists going slower than we are."

We pass cows, black, tan, brown, and white.

"So, you going to become a truck driver?" Jeff says. He doesn't give me time to answer. "Not bloody likely. Yeah, it takes a whole different mindset, a whole different set of priorities and all that crap. What would I do [without trucking]? Flipping burgers is not for me. I don't know if I could sit in one space for too long, I'd get bored too easy. Unless you're like me and you have to do this because you don't have another choice, why would you do this?"

In the eastbound lane we see a man pedalling a bike. He is wearing skin-tight cycling clothes, a yellow shirt and black shorts. He is pulling a lightweight trailer with his racing bike.

"He must have a lot more nerve than I do," says Jeff. "I've seen too many idiot drivers. There are many drivers who go down the road and don't care about anybody but themselves, so-called professional drivers who drive like idiots. I'm not lumping all the four-wheelers as bad – there are just as many bad truck drivers. They've got this humongous piece of equipment, and it doesn't stop that fast. But I've been passed on a totally blind curve in Ontario – by

four-wheelers and truckers both – and I couldn't see
what's coming and neither could the guy passing me. I
guess he figures I've got brakes. That kind of attitude really
rankles me."

We hit the Alberta border at 1:24 p.m. local time.

Jeff says, "Home sweet home."

Not far up the road, the lights are flashing at the inspection station. Jeff tugs his seat belt over his shoulder and
buckles it.

"That's the first one all trip," he says, "but there'll be
more in B.C. Those people are always open, that's why they
call it B.C. – it stands for Bring Cash. They're a little bit
hard on us. When you go into B.C., it's like you're living in
a different country."

We pass through the rolling scale. We get the yellow
light marked "Ahead Slowly." And we're off. Jeff unsnaps
his seat belt.

"There, I can take that off again. I don't wear seat belts
in a truck. I don't like anything that infringes on my
freedom – I guess that's why I'm a truck driver – and seat
belts do that, too. But in all honesty, I'd say seat belts are a
good thing. I just don't wear one. If you're going to hit
something so hard, I don't think a seat belt's going to help.
Your load's coming through anyway."

He makes a slicing motion across his neck, and I recall
the stories I've read about inertia's deadly effects, about cargo
piercing the thin trailer wall then cutting a swath through a
cab. There are safety cages on some trucks designed to keep
speeding cargo at bay, but most trucks don't have them.

Apropos of nothing, Jeff says, "I might go golfing when I get home. Drag the wife out and say, 'It's time to go golfing, dear.'"

We stop at an Esso on the outskirts of Medicine Hat. Rey takes the wheel now. We're a few hours outside of Calgary. We pass bales of fresh-cut hay. Rey looks at the grasses as we pass: "The yellow flowers are clover and the purple are alfalfa."

The road is straight, the traffic is nil. Rey grabs a pouch from the dash compartment, removes his sunglasses and begins to clean them, spraying the lenses with a solution and wiping them with a soft cloth.

We were talking about minutiae; about how Rey gets a fuel discount from Reimer – one-third less than the pump price, these days – that has kept his cost fixed for about eight years; about how Rey likes runs to Texas best because of the Mexican restaurants; about how he likes the chuck-wagon races – "the chucks" – at the Calgary Stampede; about how he thinks the mad-cow scare was a joke.

We pass a cow pasture of black grazers. "Those cows don't look too mad, do they? They look very happy."

We roll over a hill at 5:04 p.m., and I can make out a line above the horizon that I recognize as the Rocky Mountains. Rey leans forward and hugs the wheel as if it's his fat dance partner, his arms in an exaggerated O, his hands barely reaching around to grasp each other.

There is lightning to the west, and the big sky over Calgary is a mix of menace and cheer. You can see channels of each in the panorama. You can also see the Calgary skyline to the northwest. It's a dark silhouette, a foreboding visage, not the gleaming, shining place I'd seen so many times before.

And we're stuck in traffic. I see, in the snarl, a scrap truck with the same dangerous goods code, Class 8, that Rey's truck is bearing. It is filled with old car batteries and rusty paint cans and car radiators. We head for the city's southern outskirts in an attempt to avoid rush-hour traffic. But it's 5:30 p.m. and our escape route is soon foiled by a line of cars and trucks crawling so slowly that the bugs bouncing off the windshield are living to bounce again and again.

Says Rey: "We sometimes hit patches of them – skeeters, whatever – and they just plaster the windshield. They plug up the bug screen. Everything that's facing forward is just covered. You'll notice your water temperature will start to climb because the grill is covered in bugs and there's not enough airflow."

At this moment, there is no airflow. Traffic isn't moving.

"This is just crazy," says Rey. "These poor folks, they drive with it every day."

In a moment, we are driving through a hailstorm. The temperature, according to the dashboard gauge, drops from thirty degrees Celsius to thirteen degrees Celsius in about ten minutes. The hail is the size of large peas for a moment – "just big enough to dent something," says Rey, fearing for his truck – but it lets up before causing any visible damage, nicely cleaning the bug carcasses from the windshield in the process.

The hail is rain now, the mountains back in view. And we're moving faster through the foothills, the gridlock abating.

Jeff sticks his head through the curtain.

"By golly," he says. "I'd like to live up here. Then I'd think I'd died and gone to heaven, perhaps."

We're in the highlands west of Calgary, near Bragg Creek, where the *Lonesome Dove* TV series was shot.

We pass Redwood Meadows Golf and Country Club, where we see a minivan pull out of the club too quickly, swerving into our path unexpectedly before correcting its heading.

Rey laughs: "That's nice – one too many wobbly pop after the game."

Says Jeff: "I hope I get good enough to play in there someday. I'll have to buy a Rolex first, get a haircut, buy a new bag. It's kind of expensive. You've got to look the part."

Says Rey: "I'll come and caddy for you."

We shut down for supper around six-thirty, parking beside a truck that had dropped a pile of grain in the rocky parking lot, where dozens of gophers were now feasting in a pack of greed. As we walk into the restaurant, we see a truck labelled "Lightspeed Logistics."

"That's another one of them outfits with people from the other side of the ocean. How do you call 'em? New Canadians? I saw one of their drivers. He was wearing a turban," says Jeff.

Says Rey: "He was wearing a toque, eh?"

"Yeah. They call them Lightspeed because they drive at lightspeed."

In the restaurant – the usual place with booths filled with two-man teams and one-man operations and the occasional family – a trucker walks in with a Thermos the size of a small garbage can.

"Now that's a big Thermos," says Jeff. "He should be good until Vancouver – or maybe Toronto."

Rey and Jeff eat steak dinners. I opt for unmemorable fish and chips. We're back on the road, after meal, bill, bathroom, and phone calls, in forty-five minutes.

The sun is out now, the horizon squint-inducing, the roadside dotted with billboards for golf resorts and ski hills. And then there are the mountains.

"People come from all over the world to see that view," says Jeff.

That view is the Canadian Rockies stretching out across a windshield, the mighty profile of their jagged peaks back-lit by a falling sun. That view increases real-estate prices and spurs tourism and inspires roadside cyclists in skin-tight suits.

There are horses grazing by the roadside, mist coming off the pasture, snow gracing the mountaintops. As we breeze into Banff National Park, we are greeted by a deer hustling back into the bush, repelled by a roadside fence that was built to cut down on roadkill. Before the fence, elk would often find their way to the tarmac, where they'd be fed by tourists or killed by traffic. Vehicle-animal collisions are an ever-increasing problem in North America. In booming Alberta, for instance, they rose 80 per cent from 1992 to 2003.

Thousands of kilometres southeast of here, in 2000, biologist Matt Aresco, one of North America's foremost authorities on preventing those collisions, stumbled upon what he considers his life's work while driving on a highway near his Florida home. He began to notice one dead turtle, then another. In a third of a mile, he saw about twenty turtle carcasses on the side of the road. He parked his truck and got out to assess the damage on the shoulder. That first day he found the remains of about ninety dead turtles. This was especially disturbing for Aresco because he is, by trade, a turtle biologist. He'd been fascinated by turtles since he was a child, in awe of their ancient magnificence. And now he was seeing what he would later describe as a wildlife graveyard on Highway 27, just two miles from the semi-detached house he rents near the shore of Lake Jackson.

"I couldn't stand even driving that section of road with the amount of carnage there was on that stretch," he says over the line from his Florida home. "I had to do something about it. Really, since then, it's become an obsession to not only temporarily keep animals from being killed but solve the problem in the long term."

The problem was this: On that short stretch of road, Aresco would later calculate, two thousand turtles were dying per mile per year, making it the deadliest road in the world for the shelled reptiles. Aresco found that 95 per cent of turtles attempting to cross the highway were killed as they entered the highway; and the overwhelming majority of the other 5 per cent didn't make it past the first two lanes of traffic. While animals like bobcats and squirrels have the advantage of quickness, turtles are simply too slow to avoid the wrath of steel wheels. Using a statistical device known as a probability model, Aresco determined that the chances of a turtle successfully traversing the highway was 32 per cent in 1977 and, thanks to a 162 per cent increase in traffic volume, almost nil by 2001.

His temporary solution was the installation of a twenty-inch-high silt fence – basically a piece of green synthetic fabric commonly used on construction sites attached to a series of stakes that runs the length of the perilous stretch of road. The fence halted much of the death, diverting most of the turtles and the small mammals who also died in numbers. The root of the problem is harder to fix. The highway was built decades ago, when environmental regulations were far more lax. It bisects the lake, dividing what was once a single body of water into two separate bodies that are connected by exactly one culvert that burrows beneath the highway. Lake Jackson, which was formerly known by the native word Okeeheepkee, or "disappearing water," is filled with sinkholes that consume much of the water during dry spells. There are times, known as drydowns, when one side of the once-unified body dries out while the other side does not. This causes a mass migration of yellow-bellied sliders and Florida cooters and gopher tortoises, among the lengthy list of turtle species, along with various snakes and lizards and salamanders and beavers and river otters and nine-banded armadillos, to name only a short list of Florida's teeming tropical fauna. Some of the animals travel safely beneath the road through the culvert, and some of them elude the fence and traverse the road to rare success. For turtles, their only chance at survival is a statistical fluke. A lucky turtle, Aresco says, might have the front of its shell clipped by a tire.

"Suddenly there's a downward force on the front of the shell, and the turtle actually shoots off the road like a hockey puck. It'll shoot off the road sometimes thirty or forty feet. And if it pulled its head in in time, it'll be all right. It's just scraped up. But other times the head will just get crushed when that happens. And when the trucks come, it's all over. There's not much chance. What's amazing is, for as big as some of these turtles are – it's a fourteen-inch turtle with a domed shell, a really large five to seven pounds – but with the amount of traffic, if one of them gets hit, within an hour you wouldn't even know a turtle had been there. You might look really closely and see a mark on the road, and then if you get out and walk you'll find bits of bone fragments with attached skin and bone spread a quarter mile down the road. I've heard comments from people that really don't know the situation, 'Well, I drive that road all the time, and I don't see any dead turtles.' A lot of it just is hidden from the general public because these animals get totally destroyed. They're in a hundred pieces spread out down the road. I found a bobcat that was hit just a few days ago and it had gotten hit at night, so by the time I got up there in the morning, you couldn't even tell it was a carcass."

"It was just this flat piece of fur," he says. "So I got out and peeled it up, and it was a whole big bobcat that was flattened. I had to peel it off the road. When snakes get hit, the highway surface is sort of a porous kind of asphalt, it's not smooth. You actually have to use a paint scraper to get them up because they're completely embedded into these little pockets in the surface of the highways."

Aresco takes a deep breath.

"There's something about these really long-lived animals. Turtles sort of deserve a different degree of respect just because they've been around so long," he says. "They've been around pretty much unchanged for 300 million years and it's mostly due to the shell. The shell protects them. It's just ironic now that with all the hazards they face, man-caused hazards, that that shell is no protection at all. They've been around so long and a lot of species in a lot of areas are being wiped out systematically by habitat loss, habitat fragmentation from roads, and trucks. I have a photo of me walking along the 27, carrying a big snapping turtle, and someone took the photo of me right when a really big eighteen-wheeler stacked with pallets was going by. And then you can see all this eighteen-wheeler traffic in the southbound lane, so it makes it look like just wall-to-wall trucks. And it gives a good sense of how incredibly busy that highway is. And that was taken at two o'clock in the afternoon.

"I've come to hate the road. I love the lake, and I love working with the turtles, but the road itself I just hate it. And I hate the traffic on it. The worst thing is when you're out there and you see a turtle in the road and it's rush-hour traffic. And you're standing there on the side of the road, watching a turtle that's twenty, thirty, or forty years old, out in the middle of traffic. And there's nothing you can do. You just have to hope it doesn't get hit and almost all of the time it does, and it gets destroyed right in front of you. It's just awful."

Aresco's long-term solution is still in the developmental stage. It is a series of four culverts, separated by about four hundred to five hundred feet, that will lie beneath a specially designed wall that will make it nearly impossible for even the most ambitious animal to amble up from the lake onto the highway. The project still needs approval from local government, not to mention federal funding for a price tag that is estimated at $3.4 million. In the meantime, he spends his days monitoring and maintaining the temporary fence, which gets washed out in floods and trampled by the biggest turtles, the Florida softshells, and saving thousands of animals from sure death. He tags the softshells for research purposes, and so that hunters who harvest the reptiles for their prized meat reconsider their catch. Aresco's tags, a stainless-steel band he notches into the shells, read: Return $ Reward, followed by his name and phone number.

The money he pays, all out of his own pocket, depends on the person. "If I think I can get it for ten bucks, I'll try and get it for ten bucks. I've had to give a guy twenty-five." As it is, he's out there twice a day, in late morning and late afternoon, when the turtles are more active. He's out there more after rain storms that tend to knock down the fence, and during droughts. He's out there because most of the animals don't find the culvert unless they happen to wander into it. Turtles appear to have no memory of its existence, so if they happen to be south of the culvert and turn north along the fence, they'll keep walking and walking and never find their way to the water. Aresco says that's the reason the project requires culverts every four hundred or five hundred feet.

"The key is the animals have to see ambient light on the other side for them to walk through," he says. "Most animals hesitate to enter a three or four-foot diameter pipe that's completely dark. Snakes will probably do it and maybe some frogs, but as far as some of the larger animals go, the turtles and the alligators and the mammals, most of them are active during the day and need to see light."

Indeed, his home being Florida, he has encountered, alive and dead, about forty alligators during his tenure at the lake, including a ten-foot-long adult that regularly swims near the culvert. But he betrays not an ounce of fear for his safety.

"No. The highway itself is more dangerous than any-thing. The amount of truck traffic on that highway is incredible. It's a major truck route from I-10 up into Georgia and Alabama. A lot of the truckers come up I-75 through the heart of Florida, and if they're going into Alabama and the other side of Florida, they'll get on I-10 and then onto Highway 27."

The carnage, though his data tells him that only 1 per cent of the turtles he encounters are now roadkill, continues. He figures he has saved about 8,500 turtles with the temporary fences. But certain turtles can climb the fence, and many still do. The softshells simply lean on it and push it over. The smaller musk turtles, which grow to be palm-sized as adults, have sharp claws that make them excellent scalers of fabric fences.

Sometimes it's not only the animals that meet their demise. Animals in the road are safety hazards. In Fort Myers, Florida, a well-intentioned mother pulled over to help a turtle cross a busy highway; she was killed. On I-75, Aresco says, a turtle got clipped, hockey-puck style, and shot through a motorist's windshield, landing in the passenger seat next to the stunned driver. Both man and beast were unharmed.

Aresco's project is just one of hundreds around a continent on which human development impinges ever more frequently on the habitats of so many species. There are salamander tunnels in Massachusetts that have replaced the need for voluntary bucket brigades that used to stop traffic along a particular street to help migrating spotted salamanders cross without harm and continue to their mating grounds. California has corridors for cougars, crossings that help maintain genetic diversity of the far-ranging animals. Alligator Alley, the trans-Florida stretch of highway, is ringed with chain-link fence that is never interrupted and underpasses that prevent gators and endangered panthers from making a deadly dash. There are thirty-six tunnels to facilitate the reptiles' range. In Florida's Marion County, where Highway 75 interrupts terrain that is home to bobcats and opossums, a fifty-three-foot-wide overpass was built in 2000 that is lined with native trees and bedded with natural ground cover. Hikers use the trail by day; animals tend to take it over after dusk.

Banff is the world's only national park with a major highway running through it, so by the mid-1980s, officials at Parks Canada, disturbed by the frequency of roadkill and accidents caused by attempts to avoid it, started to erect fences, eight feet high apiece, on either side of the road. They also built twenty-two underpasses and two overpasses, the latter both 164 feet wide. It took time for the animals to adapt to the new routes; the first year post-construction a black bear and a cougar used the passages, once each. But soon enough researchers noticed a 96 per cent decrease in traffic-related mortality in the park's hoofed animals. Studying the users of the crossways is relatively simple thanks to motion-sensing cameras that photograph each passerby and track pads that preserve imprints of animal footprints. As a *National Geographic* article noted, one research assistant "was even caught on camera hiding behind a mound while a grizzly lumbered across the overpass and strolled safely away from the highway."

Aresco, a forty-two-year-old Ph.D., dreams of a similar moment of satisfaction, but his project has a long way to go. He can wait. It took him most of two years to get the Department of Transportation to recognize the problem and spend $125,000 on a feasibility study. In northern Florida, a hunting-and-fishing culture where a lot of citizens don't consider the preservation of turtles as a matter of grand importance, there are those who would scoff at that sum and suggest it could be better used, say, defending the homeland from terrorists.

"There's been a lot of local support . . . But there's a couple of county commissioners who are trying to argue it's a waste of money. And they really do it for political hay. If they can use it to their advantage, they'll do it. They're always looking for issues that might play well for their supporters."

Back on the Trans-Canada, Jeff is thinking about the truck driver's least favourite season. It is not the season of snow and ice.

"In the summertime, when it's peak tourist season, it's a little more strenuous, a little more stressful," says Jeff. "There's so many of 'em and they're doing forty-five miles per hour. You've just got to sit back and enjoy the scenery."

Jeff's phone rings and he takes a call from his wife. His cellular bill was $168 last month. As he talks, he points to a caribou by the railroad tracks.

"That caribou must have been eating grain that had fallen off a train car," he says after he bids his wife good night. We cross into B.C. at about nine-thirty. We pass rushing Sherbrooke Creek, flatbeds hauling plastic pipes, a Volvo tractor hauling an excavator.

On a steep decline, Jeff switches on the engine brake and gears down. We pull into a roadside staging area for a mandatory brake check.

Says Jeff: "I think I'm going to water the horses." He doesn't actually check the brakes. "I checked them stopping here. They work."

Jeff fills out his logbook and says: "This hill here, one needs to have a lot of respect for it. It's a 6 per cent grade, 8 per cent grade. You're sure not going to make the curves if you do it too fast. This short stretch of road before Golden, B.C., is notorious for accidents. I'm always of the opinion that it's not the road that kills people, it's the people who kill people."

We're rolling again, and it's here we pass the first runaway lane on the Trans-Canada. When the downhill road sweeps left, the runaway lane is the gravel fork on the right designed to be taken by truckers whose brakes are failing. The arrester bed, as it's known, amounts to a deep pit of gravel, which, along with gravity, will theoretically stop an out-of-control truck. But there've been instances when the gravel freezes and the runaway lane acts as more of a ramp than a parachute. Trucks go off the end of the things and crash. And there are truckers who, even in the worst of circumstances, won't opt for the bail-out feature. In some U.S. states, after all, there is a re-grooming fee levied when the gravel is disturbed. It's not unheard of for a driver to take his chances with a high-speed corner rather than pay that fee.

We pass bighorn rams, five of them, standing on the

road unperturbed by the noisy interruptions of mechanical beasts.

"Funny – I've never heard of anyone hitting a ram, ever," says Jeff.

The Trans-Canada Highway isn't a state-of-the-art interstate or an *autobahn*, but it's a big improvement over its earlier incarnations. One of the few men who can tell you this with the weight of experience is Ross Mackie, with whom I later visit in a boardroom of his transportation company. His grandfather effectively started the company in 1928, when he bought a single truck to transport the fruits of his labour on a farm near Oshawa. He grew tomatoes that ended up in Campbell's soup and cattle that terminated at the Toronto stockyards. Mackie's father, Merlin, was the driver. And he soon bought a second truck and combined the family farm with a little trucking on the side in slower periods.

By the 1930s and 1940s, farmhouses along the shore of Lake Ontario were being either demolished or relocated to make way for what would become Canada's busiest highway, the 401. Merlin Mackie made a business out of that. And when that work wound down, he started moving the furniture for folks whose houses were staying put.

Young Ross, at age fifteen, was, in his own words, "a hellraiser." Expelled from school, his father put him to work.

"I was really truck-crazy," he says. "I loved the trucks. I got my licence when I was sixteen, but I was already driving things I shouldn't have been."

In 1951, when Ross was seventeen, he and his dad took a load of furniture to Vancouver.

"That was a really big deal because the Trans-Canada Highway, there were sections of it that were gravel roads and there was no Rogers Pass," he says. "There were areas you'd get stuck in and you'd have construction or farmers towing you if you had some bad luck.

"We made the trip to Vancouver and the truck was under-powered and it didn't have air brakes and when we went through the mountains in B.C. on the old highway – down around Cranbrook and Trail and in those areas – there were two summits you had to go over and it would take you three hours to go forty miles. My dad was really scared. When we got to Vancouver, we unloaded the furniture and he said, 'I'm going to try and sell the truck and trailer and we'll go home on the train.'"

Merlin Mackie's fears weren't unwarranted. The pass is named after its discoverer, A.B. Rogers, a railroad surveyor who was commissioned by the Canadian Pacific Railway to find a route between the Selkirk Mountains, which stood between Calgary and Vancouver and posed what had been for decades an impassable, inhospitable barrier. Routes through the other mountain ranges that made the railway such a testament to will and engineering – Alberta's Rockies and British Columbia's Purcells and Monashees – had been surveyed decades earlier. But the Selkirks were a true no man's land. Indians had avoided their harsh climate, their ten-metres-per-winter snowfall, and the infamous snow slides that snapped one-hundred-year-old trees like a child snaps a twig. Rogers was offered as incentive for his formidable task both a five-thousand-dollar reward and what would these days be termed the naming rights of his route. And though he never collected the cash, his intrepid foray into what was then untouched wilderness revealed in 1881 what had long been hoped for – a relatively direct route through the Selkirks that would connect the westernmost member of Confederation with the rest of the big Dominion.

Still, it took decades before man came close to managing the avalanches that claimed so many lives. About 250 railroad workers were killed during the CPR's three-decade run over Rogers Pass, including sixty-two men in one 1910 disaster. Eventually the threat of the snowslides and the engineers' inability to limit their ravages, despite the building of numerous snowsheds that deflected falling snow away from the tracks, forced engineers to abandon the pass in favour of boring an eight-kilometre hole through Mount Macdonald that became known as the Connaught Tunnel, the longest such structure in Canada.

Armed with better technology, it took nearly six years, from 1956 to 1962, to build a road over Rogers Pass. And it's still a battle against nature. Parks Canada maintains what it claims is the world's largest mobile avalanche control program in the continuing effort to keep the highway open. In 2003, seven Alberta high-school students on a ski trip were killed in a massive avalanche in the pass near Revelstoke. It was the worst avalanche in the area in a couple of decades.

The plan that might have taken the family abruptly out of the trucking business never unfolded. Merlin Mackie's truck was beyond saleable. It had hydraulic brakes that were outmoded for mountain driving. It had no sleeper berth ("You had a pillow on the bench seat," remembers Ross). So they drummed up an eastbound load of furniture and rolled back across the northland.

"On the way home my dad said to me, 'If I bought a bigger truck with air brakes and more power, would you be interested in doing this?' I was gung-ho. So he bought a new truck – the make of it was a White – and a new Trailmobile trailer. I thought I'd died and gone to heaven."

Ross, at age seventeen, started running to Vancouver and Halifax and anywhere, including Alaska and Yukon in the dead of winter.

"The way I tell it, I knew right then that my dad never liked me. I hit weather that was forty below, fifty below. On that trip, from Edmonton to Whitehorse, it was all gravel road."

But the young trucker discovered a country of burgeoning business opportunities. He discovered, in Whitehorse, the unlikely first in what would become a staple of the company's business. An American businessman who'd driven there in his black Lincoln found his car broken down and nary a mechanic who could help him fix it. Mackie, fresh from dumping a load of furniture, hauled it to Edmonton; a half-century later he'd be hauling Formula One cars from Montreal to Mexico.

Theirs was a family business. Ross's mother, Amanda, used to have the washing machine in the dispatch office. She'd do laundry while she answered the phone and typed up invoices on an old Underwood.

But the Trans-Canada, though the young man loved plying it, didn't always reciprocate the affection. In Saskatchewan, he remembers, hard rain would turn the road to what the truckers called gumbo. Mackie slid off the road into a ditch one day; it took the kindness of a local farmer to pull the truck out. And it couldn't have been more than fifteen minutes back in action that he lost control again; it spurred his father, riding shotgun, to give the boy a slap in the head. The roads would close during blizzards. "You'd just park your truck and hope you had enough fuel to keep idling," says Mackie. The highway, when it was dry, was made of gravel, mostly, although it was paved around some cities. From Hearst to Longlac, driving through the uninhabited Canadian Shield, the job sometimes didn't seem so appealing.

"We used to refer to it as The Stretch," says Mackie. "In the dead of winter it would reach forty or fifty below. When you left Hearst, there was a checkpoint there and you'd give them your licence number and your company, and if you didn't make it to the middle checkpoint, they'd come to look for you so you didn't freeze to death."

Sometimes, though, it felt like they'd never come. One winter night, to wit, Mackie announced his intention to brave the stretch in the wee hours. He was young and knew it all, he says, and though a few of the veteran drivers urged him to reconsider – to park his truck in Hearst and head out at first light – he didn't take their advice.

"It was probably forty-five below that night. The steering started to freeze up on it, and I couldn't steer it, and then the shift linkage was freezing too. I couldn't go any farther. So I wrapped myself in furniture blankets, because I figured the truck was going to quit soon. And I was almost freezing to death. Luckily, one of the guys from the department of highways came out in a pickup truck and rescued me, and he gave me a lecture. The older guys were giving me good advice and I didn't take it.

"I don't remember much more about it, but I know I was scared. You're out there alone and there's no vehicles coming or going. The heaters then, they weren't any good. That truck was so bad, so terribly cold in that truck. I eventually bought a little propane heater and bolted it to the floor, and then I mounted a tank on the back of the cab. But that left your skin so dried, it was terrible. It was warm, but you were like a dried prune. And you had to be careful. Sometimes you'd light it and you'd almost blow the windows out."

Jeff is driving in climate-controlled comfort now, and we glimpse Golden, an industrial valley town that shimmers in the evening. And on Golden's other side, as advertised, we meet an open inspection station.

"Sure as heck they're going to want to see my paperwork," mumbles Jeff.

As we wait in line for inspection, Jeff tells the story of a disgruntled trucker who, apparently fed up with the prodding of the inspection-station authorities, entered the facility with a tire iron with which he wreaked considerable havoc.

There is no such drama at this stop. We are waved through the scale without being beckoned to produce the paperwork. A little up the road, we pass a sign: "Fixtranscanada.org." The website, I find out later, is a grassroots protest of what its creator insists are the below-standard conditions of the road from the B.C. side of the Alberta border to Salmon Arm. It's a sentiment shared by the truckers who ply the pan-national highway. There has been talk of twinning the highway, making it two lanes each way from coast to coast, bringing it up to the standards of your average U.S. interstate, and with better rest-stop facilities. But the project, which would ideally separate westbound traffic from eastbound with a substantial buffer of trees and earth, will cost untold billions.

The head-on accidents will keep happening.

"You see a wreck just about every other day," says Jeff.

You see a wreck just about every other day, perhaps, because so much changes when you're driving in the mountains. For Andy Roberts, an acknowledged expert in the art of alpine transportation, driving trucks in British Columbia's rare air is a birthright. He learned here and made mistakes here and learned to respect, above all, gravity here. Flatlanders, as Roberts calls the sojourning citizens of

non-mountainous regions who make it their business to
travel the passes and switchbacks he's known all his life,
don't have an appreciation for the power of gravity.

"A lot of these guys, we see 'em all the time, they come
out from Saskatchewan and Alberta and they have the
expectation they can go down a mountain at ninety kilometres an hour," says Roberts, laughing. "And, of course,
they're using an amazing amount of brakes and they're
building up an amazing amount of heat, to the point where
the brakes are actually catching on fire. We've seen 'em literally light the tires on fire. That doesn't happen that frequently, but it can happen."

It can happen, but not to Roberts and his attentive students at the Mountain Transport Institute in Castlegar, B.C.
At MTI, would-be mountain-savvy truckers take an eight-
week course that teaches them much of what they need to
know to become employable, efficient, and, above all,
long-living drivers. And the key to much of the teaching is
to build an understanding of the physics of the industry.
Trucks are heavy, legally as heavy as 140,000 pounds in
Canada, which allows bigger trucks than the United States,
where 80,000-pound rigs are the standard. Stopping is
never as easy as pushing the brake pedal. The brake pedal,
after all, activates the truck's service brakes, which are
ill-suited to downhill conditions. Service brakes heat up
quickly and cool slowly, and hot brakes perform less impressively as they get hotter.

But many novice drivers don't seem to understand this,

and so the single biggest mistake most truck drivers make, Roberts says, is going downhill too speedily. The goal of the responsible mountain driver is to descend even the steepest grades without so much as stepping on the brake pedal.

"We always run the hills like we don't have brakes," Patrick Peters, an MTI instructor, has said. "That way when you need them, they're there. Then, the worst thing that can happen is if we lose a gear, we come to a stop and do it over. The engine gets you up the hill and the engine gets you down the hill."

Selecting gears – letting the engine get you up and down the hill – is not unlike selecting golf clubs, although not exactly the same thing. If you've ever watched a professional golfer hem and haw over the comparative merits of, say, a nine iron or a pitching wedge, you've watched the sporting equivalent of drying beige paint. Truckers choose gears more quickly out of necessity. To hesitate is to lose momentum. To lose momentum is to use more fuel than is necessary. Shifting isn't rocket science; it can be mastered by the vast majority of drivers with repetition and experience. But it's complicated enough that a lot of new trucks come with automatic transmissions as an option. Big trucking companies, always looking for ways to make the job easier as they scrape the bottom of the labour pool, opt in. And even some experienced truckers rave about the convenience of automatic shifting, especially in stop-and-go traffic, when manual shifting, in a big truck or in a little car, can be tedious.

Roberts says the drivers of automobiles, many of whom enjoy the luxury of automatic transmission in their 2,500-pound Hondas, can't appreciate the extent of gravity's pull. Most cars have a horsepower-to-weight ratio that makes the climbing of a lot of grades almost imperceptible. The engine doesn't labour. A car set in cruise control barely registers a note of extra effort. Even the big hills in British Columbia, the 8 per cent and 9 per cent graders, are no match for a peppy Honda Civic. It's the truckers and the cyclists, says Roberts, who truly understand the extent of the Earth's pull.

"A 1 or 2 per cent grade in your car, you don't even notice it. But as soon as you're on your bicycle, it becomes very apparent. So if I put you in a truck with 140,000 pounds and send you to a 7 per cent grade, it's like a bicycle. It decelerates very quickly when you're going up and it accelerates very quickly when you're headed down. So your gear-shifting techniques have to be adjusted, not a little bit, but a lot, in order to keep the vehicle moving and keep it under control."

Keeping it under control isn't always easy. Jackknifing happens when the trailer gets going faster than the tractor and takes over in the race, and what regular listener of any North American city's rush-hour traffic report doesn't hear the words "jackknifed tractor-trailer" and "backing things up" in the same sentence at least once every couple of weeks? Mountains, though, aren't an excuse most urban traffic backer-uppers can cite. But mountains – going down them, specifically – are a frequent cause of jackknifed vehicles.

One way prudent truckers avoid calamity is to use an engine brake, commonly referred to as a Jake Brake after the Jacobs Company of Bloomfield, Connecticut. It's an engine retarder, not a physical brake, which is activated, not with a pedal, but with a flip of a switch on the dash. It essentially turns the diesel engine into an air compressor, holding back the truck instead of propelling it. Some of the most powerful Jake Brakes have as much as six-hundred-horsepower of holdback. Disc brakes are available, but not widely used. They're more expensive, but they're far more efficient than the drum-based models that are commonplace. They don't overheat as easily and, according to the boasts of manufacturers, bring stopping distances more in line with those of automobiles. Still, no matter the technology, Roberts doesn't encourage hitting the brake pedal.

"On a short hill they'll get away with that," he says. "But in British Columbia, we have hills that are ten miles long. So if I start off the top of that hill and go that long in too high of a gear, and I have to rely on my service brakes to keep my speed in check, I build up too much heat in my service brakes. The drums expand. And eventually I can lose my brakes entirely, and now I'm in a runaway situation.

"Or at the very least I get my brakes heated up and if I need to make an emergency stop I probably couldn't."

That means truckers need to pick a low enough gear, sometimes as low as third gear on an eighteen-speed transmission, and go at a slow enough speed, sometimes in the range of twenty-five kilometres an hour, to descend safely.

In British Columbia it's recommended that vehicles descending hills at less than forty kilometres an hour turn on their four-way flashers, their hazard lights. In other provinces, driving with the four-way flashers activated is illegal. Local knowledge is important, not to mention scarce.

"I learned from some of the old-timers, and when you learn from them, you learn how to do it right," he says. "These are guys who'd been doing it a long, long time, back when they had really underpowered trucks. It's in my blood. This is just where I live and what I do. To be able to share that with people and get them to have a thorough understanding of it is really important. Our drivers learn they have to be looking down the road and making decisions ahead of time."

I ask Roberts how he decides which gear to select.

"Going down a hill, there's different stories depending who you ask. Some use the same gear you came up the hill with or one gear lower than when you came up a hill. The problem is a mountain isn't exactly equal on both sides," he says. "If you're familiar with your truck and your load, when you look at the sign at the top and it says an 8 per cent or 7 per cent grade, you may already have a good idea of what gear that would be in your truck. That just comes with experience. If you have absolutely no idea at all, what I recommend is you start off the top of the hill and you let the truck teach you what gear it wants to go down the hill in. If I left the top of the hill I know I'm going to be at least in third gear, and then, with the engine brake on I would take my foot off the throttle and watch what the truck does. If I'm in third gear and it's sitting at 1,400 rpm and holding, I can go to a maximum 2,100 rpm in my truck. So I know I can pick up another gear and just let gravity pick up the speed. Fourth gear, maybe I'm holding at 1,900 or 2,000 rpm. I'll just sit there all the way down the hill. I want to find the gear that's going to keep me as close to 2,100 rpm without going over."

The magic number is 2,100 rpm, in this case, because, says Roberts, "That's what the engine is rated at. Any higher than that and you'll damage the engine."

There are other ways to make trucks more at home in the Rocky Mountain highs and lows. There are electronic driveline retarders and hydraulic driveline retarders that can reduce stopping distances by a significant percentage. There are exhaust brakes, which work on a similar principle to engine brakes by restricting the flow of exhaust gases and thereby increasing backpressure in the engine, which in turn increases resistance for the engine's pistons and slows the vehicle. Some truckers run a combination of the two, and they'll end up with seven hundred or eight hundred horsepower of holdback. They can descend faster because they have more stopping power. But every advantage has a price. Retarders of all kinds are harder on tires because the drive tires are essentially holding the truck back. They add weight to the truck, which means there's less leeway for payload.

"There's a balance to all this stuff," says Roberts. "You just don't put on a bunch of holdback and race down the hill because you'll be putting tires on way more often," says Roberts.

Labatt Breweries used to run its own fleet of super-trains from the Kokanee Brewery in Creston to Vancouver. Leaving Creston, the trucks encountered the Salmo-Creston summit and, with it, one of the steepest, longest grades in the province. On an average year, three trucks employ the runaway lane and the arrester bed. To avoid that fate, the brewer put engine brakes and hydraulic driveline retarders on its trucks.

"They used to get quite a few trucks coming out of the prairies and those guys would look at the Labatts trucks and say, 'He's a supertrain and I'm a supertrain. I've never been down this hill. I'll follow him.' Well, of course, they had all this additional braking power. And they eventually had to put signs on the back of their trailers, 'This vehicle is equipped with a retarder. Please do not try to keep up.' These guys from the prairies were burning their brakes up because they didn't have the same amount of holdback."

Guys from the prairies still try to keep up, still burn out their brakes. Oregon is the only U.S. state that posts speed limits by truck weight. Sometimes they end up out of control, their brakes useless, thousands of pounds of cargo chasing them down a mountain. Escape ramps, steep off-road upslopes located in the midst of particularly hard-to-handle downslopes, are designed for such moments of panic. The ramps are long driveways of deep gravel, also known as arrester beds, which will ideally halt the downhill progress of a runaway truck. They don't always work: Roberts has seen truckers run through the ends of the beds and crash. And the deep gravel, which is supposed to provide a soft landing, gets significantly harder in winter.

"Our biggest challenge in driving conditions is temperature," Roberts says. "You may start in a valley and it'll be raining and it'll be plus-one [Celsius]. And by the time you reach the summit of that mountain pass it may be minus-ten. So your road conditions are changing constantly through that entire climb. You go from rain to slush to wet snow to dry snow. If you take a guy out in the winter and it's minus-ten and minus-twenty and the snow has been lightly sanded, the road conditions are almost as good as they are in the summer.

"But when we're right around the zero mark, we have a high moisture content in the snow. It packs and it's very slippery. They say people in Vancouver can't drive in the snow. You know why people in Vancouver can't drive in the snow? Because they have lousy snow. Really. Because when it snows there it's usually right around zero and there's high moisture content and it's extremely slippery. And they don't do it very often."

Trucker lore says the steepest hill in British Columbia is known simply as The Hill, a drop-off with 18 per cent grades that you meet driving westward on Highway 20 toward Bella Coola, where the freshwater Bella Coola River meets the saltwater of the Pacific. Roberts has never driven that road, and he laughs at the ridiculousness of the grade, which he says may be as steep as 22 per cent in some stretches; 6 per cent is what most truckers would consider a steep hill.

"The scary thing is that when I started about eighteen years ago, if I got out of line as a rookie driver, there were always a few old-timers telling me to smarten up," Roberts says. "Whether they worked for my carrier or not, it just wasn't accepted. We've seen an increase in trucks on the highway. We've seen a huge increase in driver turnover. And the scary thing is, a lot of those old-timers have either retired or are within five or ten years of retirement. There was a time when I would have told you trucks are safe, drivers are great, they'll help you out, they're reliable, they're professional. I can't say that today. I'm scared of who's coming toward me now because I don't know them and I don't know where or if they were trained and I don't know what their attitude is. And I don't know whether they just got up or they haven't slept in two days. Not that there's a lot of those guys out there, but there's a lot more than there ever used to be. It's not the odd guy. There are too many people out there who think they're professional drivers just because they get paid, not because of how they do their job."

It's 4:45 a.m. and we're nearing Kamloops, B.C., the fog obscuring our mountain view, a flatbed in front of us hauling planks that sway and shimmy. Dawn breaks slowly, soft and grey, and the greenery – in our first view of the gardener's province – is noticeably lusher, bushier, fatter than the scrub on the other side of the mountains. We pull into a scale 145 kilometres west of Vancouver. No problems.

The inspector isn't even looking at us. By 6:30 a.m., the highway is heavy with commuters. The signs above the road encourage carpooling, but most of the four-wheelers are one-man operations, BCers alone in their SUVs, Pathfinders and Trailblazers, heading to work.

But the work, in this truck, is almost done. It's just past 9:00 when we pull up at the destination. Jeff drops the trailer, we all walk inside to the office, and after Rey reports his arrival – and makes a note of the 4,436 kilometres that have been tacked onto the odometer since our Ontario departure – we're off to breakfast in the trailer-less rig.

Everybody's tired but happy. We eat pancakes not far from the hotel where Rey and Jeff will sleep the day away awaiting the load they'll take back to Calgary the next morning. By ten o'clock we are saying our goodbyes. I hop a train to Stanley Park, where I'm walking on the seawall by noon, my body still vibrating with the buzz.

6

Tourists and Other Professionals

Not twenty minutes into our journey from rural Southwestern Ontario to the San Francisco piers – from the Great Lakes to the great Pacific – a silver Honda Civic zips by on the left. A.J. McIntosh, at the wheel of his burgundy Freightliner, watches the car closely and raises his eyebrows from under the cover of his bug-eyed aviator shades. He has just begun a dissertation on the intricacies and inanities of border brokerages – he is questioning the very existence of the middlemen who, for a fee, act as a liaison between shippers and customs agents at the Canada–U.S. crossing point – but as the silver Honda speeds ahead, McIntosh interrupts his discourse with an exclamation.

"That guy's getting a blow job!" A.J. says. "Lucky bugger. I've seen two this week! I mean, she was right on his lap!"

He laughs like Santa, his shoulders shaking, his right

hand slapping the stick shift: "Now I've really lost my train of concentration."

Helen, his driving partner of six months who is sitting on the truck's lower bunk, behind the fridge and the microwave and the ten-inch TV, leans forward and taps the shoulder of the notepad-wielding intruder in the passenger seat. She is rolling her eyes at A.J. when she speaks.

"I hardly ever look down when I'm driving," she says. "Oh yeah, you see all kinds of things going down the road. About two trips ago, I was listening to the CB and all the guys were talking about this woman in an SUV. She was driving along completely naked for all the truck drivers to see. I haven't seen any of the blow jobs or anything, but the other girls who drive tell me, 'Oh yeah, you should see them.'

"Some women, they'll just flash their boobs. I've seen the boobs come out, you know, not knowing that I'm a woman truck driver, flashing the boobs at me."

A.J., a twenty-seven-year veteran of the rolling canyons, has not stopped giggling since the Honda left the horizon. It's a late-summer scorcher out there, the air conditioning is blasting and the CB is alive with chatter, but our driver speaks not a word about the weather or the status of the coming inspection station, which turns out to be closed to truck traffic. He seems bent on recounting his personal list of the greatest moments in highway exhibitionism. The list is long.

"It makes your day," he says. "I had this old guy and gal one time, a husband and wife. They were both in their late fifties or sixties, maybe. At nighttime, she had a flashlight, and she was sitting on her knees over against the passenger window and she had on, like, a red negligee of some sort, and it was pulled down low and her boobs were hanging pretty low, eh? She was playing with herself, right? And this old guy's getting his jollies, pulling up beside the truck drivers just going nuts, giving a little show and going on to the next one. But she was just so old, eh? The fat was just hanging off her. The boobs were – gravity had taken over a long time ago. It was almost funny."

Helen, who is wearing an anti-trucker wardrobe of meticulously pressed khaki slacks, a white sleeveless blouse and black flat sandals, winces and laughs. She is in her rookie season on the flasher watch but already, barely 1 per cent of the way on this drive to San Francisco and a handful of other stops on the California coast, she is wearing a look on her face that says, "I don't need this."

Before this, she spent twenty-five years as an employee of various banks. Then one day last year, after taking a trucking trip with a former boyfriend and becoming instantly enchanted with the road's allure, she quit the bank and signed up for truck-driving school, from which she emerged to pass the provincial licensing test on the first try. Although women continue to occupy a very few driver's seats – about 5 per cent according to many estimates – there is a feeling among most long-time truckers that, with the economic advantages of team driving being touted by many trucking firms, women are increasing their numbers all the time.

Putting two drivers in one truck, of course, keeps the truck moving – and therefore, in a per-mile business, keeps the money coming in – without costly but necessary respites for sleep.

"We'll drive in five-hour shifts," says A.J., "and it works out beautifully. Legally one driver can drive ten hours and then you have to take eight hours off, and then you can drive ten more again. But if you work five hours, you can take five to rest and drive another five, as long as you don't exceed the seventy hours in eight days."

Helen isn't interested in the numbers.

"I just wanted to be free, I think," Helen says. "Trucking, it seems like everybody is doing it now. You're trying to get out of a job, you get into trucking. Once you go out on a truck it's just magic."

Granted, trucking companies from the tundra to the Mexican border are complaining about the massive defections of experienced drivers who succumb to the job's many frustrations and seek alternate employment. But Helen tells of similar disenchantment in her banking career. After a quarter century of loyal service, her annual salary was $43,000. In a little more than nine months as a trucker, she says he has earned $38,000, although she acknowledges she has yet to take a holiday lasting more than a weekend.

"There's too much pressure at the bank," she says. "Even if you're answering the phone, you've got to have a certain number of referrals. I was a personal banking officer until October of 2001, when I quit. And in the September before

I quit, they set my goals for the next year, and they said, 'Okay, you're getting $10-million worth of mortgages this year.' I said, 'Yeah, but you only gave me $7.5 million last year.' And they said, 'Well, you got the $7.5 million, so now we're increasing it.' I can't say I hated it. It's just now, I found something I like doing better than banking. I miss some of the customers. But now the customers are the people at the loading dock."

Her only co-worker – who also happens to be her boss, A.J. being the owner-operator of this rig and another – is a strapping forty-something wiseacre who enjoys telling a lewd joke and teasing a neophyte. Helen is not the first of A.J.'s fresh-from-the-office protegés. A while back he trained an accountant who wanted a career change, but the accountant shared A.J.'s truck for only a few weeks before he struck out on his own. The accountant's solo foray into the U.S. heartland lasted, as A.J. remembers it, all of two weeks.

"Everybody wants to do this job," says A.J., "and then they get out here and realize it's not all what they thought it was. It's a hard job."

This, says A.J., won't exactly be a hard trip. It's a Sunday afternoon in August and the first of the team's deliveries – which include a dozen or so boxes of high-end kitchen equipment bound for San Francisco, the possessions of an engineer formerly based in Montreal and recently trans- ferred to the U.S. West Coast, and assorted packages bound for a myriad of other destinations – isn't due until Tuesday. Considering A.J., in a pinch, has made the trip in forty-four hours, this isn't exactly a rush job. Still, there are more than four thousand kilometres to cover between these Southwestern Ontario farmlands and San Francisco's foggy charms, and so we will roll, with only periodic interruptions – a museum here, a shopping excursion there – for most of the next fifty hours.

We will cross the border on the Bluewater Bridge, which links Sarnia, Ontario, with Port Huron, Michigan, and we will truck west on Interstate 69 until we join Interstate 80, the famous corridor that links New York City and San Francisco and, for long stretches in between, follows the trans-American route first laid out by the hand-cart-wheeling pioneers who settled the U.S. West.

We'll bisect the vast plains, cut through Iowa, slice Nebraska, skirt the bottom of Wyoming, climb up Utah's mountains, and fall into Nevada's flats. And we'll hit California, where stringent regulations on heavy vehicles make it the least favoured destination of so many truckers.

"It is the type of job, you're pretty free out here," A.J. says. "We have to be in San Francisco on Tuesday, but how we decide to do it between here and there, we have nobody looking over our shoulder like in a factory."

A.J. knows that his truck's whereabouts is easily monitored by his bosses at Monarch Linehaul; his truck, like most, is linked via satellite to company headquarters. But he sees the technology as more of a help than a hindrance. He used to have to call his dispatcher after every delivery, which got a little old on a busy day with a dozen different destinations. Now he simply makes note of his progress with a few taps on the keyboard and, without a phone call, without being put on hold, his status is updated.

A.J., like most owner-operators, is obsessive about limiting wear and tear on his truck. To his eye, every gear-grinding shift, every brake-pedal squeeze – they all leach money from his pocket. The transmission and the brakes are there to be preserved, not abused. Every shift, after all, brings the transmission one shift closer to being replaced; every abrupt stop takes the brakes that much closer to a service call.

A.J. is a throwback to the days when truckers once needed to be physically durable and manually dexterous and mechanically inclined; when they needed big shoulders and biceps and forearms, or at least wiry-strong ones; when they had to change their own tires. These days new trucks come with a 1-800 number for roadside assistance.

The march of technology continues. Truck companies are rolling out electronic stability control systems, already available on cars and light trucks, that can detect when a truck is poised to roll over and take steps to prevent it, including hitting the service brakes, activating the engine brake, and cutting the throttle. The system works with sensors that constantly compare the direction the steering wheel is pointing with the direction the car is heading. If a discrepancy is detected, a microcomputer calculates a solution in a fraction of a second. Considering some 58 per cent of truck fatalities are the result of a rolled tractor, technology to prevent them makes sense.

There is also adaptive cruise control, which can detect

when the vehicle ahead is slowing or stopping and apply the brakes without any input from the driver. There are blind-spot radar systems that can be mounted anywhere alongside the truck and alert drivers to the presence of traffic in places they can't humanly see. There are manufacturers that produce a lane-departure warning system, emitting a loud noise, not unlike the sound of rolling over a rumble strip, when the truck leaves its lane. And though it's handy to have around when driving in rain and fog, it is said to be useless in snow.

There are even truck companies testing the idea of a global positioning system that could survey, say, the corner a truck is approaching and, no matter the driver's careless whim, not allow the vehicle to take the corner at an inappropriate speed. And to minimize flat tires there are tire-inflation regulators that automatically adjust the tire pressure in different temperature conditions. The systems also detect blowouts, rapidly infusing a ruptured tire with air so that the driver can exit the highway without incident.

Flat tires are often a product of poor tire maintenance. Increasing one's speed from 55 mph to 65 mph, for instance, would ideally accompany an increase in tire pressure from the traditional 100 psi to 105 psi. Tires need to be rotated. The front, or drive tires, need to swap places occasionally. The driver-side tire tends to wear faster than the passenger-side counterpart because of the camber of most roads. Also, the outside treads of the tires tend to wear faster than the inside, so a simple flip of the orientation can even out the wear pattern and make for longer life.

Longevity is elusive, though. A well-cared-for set of tires can last 400,000 miles. Tires with the least rolling resistance are among the least durable, lasting somewhere between 250,000 to 300,000 miles. But their economic advantage comes in the form of fuel economy; manufacturers trumpet numbers that suggest tires with lower rolling resistance are, though less durable, cheaper per mile when fuel savings are considered.

Underinflation is a killer; a tire that's 20 per cent short of its proper pressure will cut its lifespan by some 16 per cent according to a Goodyear study, and the majority of tire failures can be chalked up to inadequate pressure. Oxidation, which turns rubber brittle and less elastic (and more prone to rupturing), takes its toll, so some trucking companies fill their tires, not with free-for-the-taking air, but with pure compressed nitrogen, which already makes up 78 per cent of the atmosphere and doesn't have oxygen's destructive bent. Auto-racing pit crews have used nitrogen to fill their tires for years, mostly because compressed nitrogen contains less moisture than compressed air. When the tire heats up, the moisture in air expands, causing unwanted increases in pressure that can affect handling.

Worn tires don't have to be thrown in a landfill. Retreading is an option with negative connotations, but it is common practice. The owners of large fleets typically retread tires twice. New tires go on the tractor, especially on the drive wheels, where traction is critical. First-time retreads are destined for duty on trailers. Second-time retreads go on trailers and on trucks known as yard mules, which are used to move trailers around a trucking company's yard.

Retreads are economically sensible. And they're also environmentally friendly. Some eighty-three litres of oil go into the production of a new truck tire. Just twenty-seven litres are used in the production of a retread, which reuses the casing of an old tire and avoids the inevitable scrapping for hundreds of thousands more miles. Scrap tires are a bane. They're ideal mosquito breeding grounds. They burn in piles and, in their smoke, distribute carcinogens to the surrounding areas. A tire fire in Hagersville, Ontario, burned for seventeen days in 1990. Another in Winchester, Virginia, burned for nine months spanning 1983 and 1984. And, when they're discarded in landfills, they won't stay buried.

The American writer John McPhee visited the world's largest pile of scrap tires near Modesto, California, and estimated there were 34 million on site. There are some 3 billion abandoned tires in the United States.

"In some places, they are six stories high, compressing themselves, densifying: at the top, tires; at the bottom, pucks," wrote McPhee, describing the Modesto heap in his book *Irons in the Fire*. "From the highest elevations of this thick and drifted black mantle, you can look east a hundred miles and see snow on the Sierra."

Truckers still have to chain their own tires, which is no desk job. In the worst of winter, especially in the mountains when the snow gets deep and the slopes are steep, tire chains are standard equipment. (Although because some companies urge their drivers to avoid icy conditions at all costs, there are veterans of the trade, twenty-year drivers, who have never strapped the iron to the rubber.) For many truckers, though, chains are a necessity – and in some parts of North America during snowfalls, a legal requirement – if not to get a load to its destination on time, then to arrive safely at the closest rest stop until conditions take a turn.

The most durable chains are made of nickel-manganese steel. Titanium-blend chains are lighter and don't last as long. They are typically applied to the tires on one or both of a standard rig's two drive axles. The back wheels of the trailer sometimes get chains to prevent it from slipping and sliding in the rig's wake, although there are those who'd say if the trailer needs chains the driver needs to pull over and wait out the weather. There are tricks of the slippery-weather trade. Experienced eyes watch the tires of the sur-rounding vehicles. If they're kicking up spray, the road is likely wet. If the road is glistening but the spray is scarce, it's probably covered in ice. Shiny tarmac on a bridge in cold weather is, odds are, icy. Bridges freeze first. Big rigs get stuck, so prepared truckers keep bags of cat litter or sand in tow to spread for traction and a tow chain, a thirty-footer or so, for quagmires that require outside assistance. It's not uncommon for drivers to pour antifreeze or rubbing alcohol under tires to melt the ice and restore grip, but those remedies can have damaging effects on rubber over time.

A.J., who is precious about the cleanliness of his truck and the longevity of its every component, would never stoop to such messy measures. And on this day, he has but a couple of rules for a first-time rider. For one, he is firm in his belief that shoes must be removed upon entering his domain. ("It's like our house," he says. "You take your shoes off at the door.") For another, anything that has touched the surface of a truck-stop parking lot is to be treated like it's been infected with bubonic plague. Says Helen, explaining why she chided me for setting my duffle down next to the truck earlier that day: "You'll see drivers emptying their pee bottles on the pavement beside their trucks. So you never, never set anything down in the parking lot."

The truck is accordingly spotless. A.J. chastises Helen for her insistence on order; he calls her "Little Miss Organization." But the farther we rolled along, the more obvious it becomes that *he* is the neat freak. Freightliners have a nickname in the business: Freightshakers. There's a joke, "What's the difference between a Jehovah's Witness and the door on a Freightliner?" and the punchline goes, "you can close the door on the Jehovah's Witness." But A.J. coddles iron, as it's called, like a gurgling baby. Witness the container of moist towelettes he keeps zip-stripped to the driver-side seat-belt buckle, a housekeeping resource with which he frequently wipes his hands or the steering wheel or the never-dusty dashboard. Witness the lack of clutter; the cleanest carpets you'll probably ever see in any vehicle that recently rolled its odometer past the 1,000,000-kilometre mark. Witness the closet full of company-logoed shirts behind the driver's seat, all of them in A.J.'s size, XL, all of them ironed in right-angled creases. And witness, too, the frequency with which A.J. brushes his teeth. From what I can figure, he puts bristle to enamel at least five times a day. He will, in the fifty-some hours of our journey, unfurl his dental-hygiene supplies at least eleven times, often, when a bathroom sink isn't in the vicinity, dipping the head of his brush into a bottle of water, applying the toothpaste, and spitting the white foam into a Ziploc bag as he drives.

As someone who has ducked his head into hundreds of cabs to interview the residents, I can tell you that all of this über-tidy behaviour isn't exactly unusual. Still, the interiors of the majority of trucks I have perused could best be described as functionally messy, their floors strewn with a layer of detritus – road atlases, travel mugs, news-papers, and shopping bags – that at one time or another serves a perfectly logical purpose. Things pile up, though, and soon, no matter one's intentions, there is an ankle-deep filing cabinet in use.

A.J., of course, has no such trouble. His atlas is filed in a mesh pocket for the driver's easy reference. His travel mug never strays from its holder. He doesn't buy newspapers. And he doesn't need to go shopping. Spending Canadian dollars on U.S. fast food can be an expensive and unhealthy business, so the truck is packed with edibles, including apparently limitless supplies of wieners from a meat-packing plant in Kitchener that isn't far from A.J.'s home. "If you go right to the factory, they sell you the seconds really cheap," A.J. says. I raise an eyebrow: If first-quality wieners have a reputation for being filled with the fruits of the abattoir's floor, what, pray tell, is contained in second-quality tubesteaks? A.J. laughs the laugh of a man who thinks he's getting the deal of the century: "They're the same as the firsts, they're just not perfect." And it isn't long after he speaks those words that A.J. is microwaving his cut-rate dogs, nuking them until they're split and blistered, and we're all digging in with Wonder buns and mustard.

When you're eating a microwaved hot dog and sipping a refrigerated cola in the passenger seat of a big rig, the chaos of the road falls away and the experience is surprisingly calming.

Helen is driving now, and she is fighting her way through Chicago-area traffic, fiddling with the atlas to nail down an alternate route around the current quagmire. She is literally and figuratively above the fray. She isn't, like the four-wheelers returning from vacation on this Sunday night, zipping from lane to lane and going nowhere. She is waiting it out, planning ahead, readying to take an exit. She is not, unlike an uppity green SUV, breaching the rumble strips and high-tailing it down the shoulder to pass a couple of hundred cars and, with the illegal progress halted by a bridge, returning to reality. She is chatting about life, her old one specifically.

"Mary, who's the bank manager, she and I are friends," says Helen. "We were more friends, actually, before she became the manager of the bank. Mary had no idea I was quitting. I told her I was taking a trucking course, but she never heard 'trucking,' she just heard 'course.' And she thought, 'Oh good, Helen took a course to update herself

at the bank.' Jill, who works with me, is going, 'Mary, she's
going to drive a truck.' And Mary said, 'What? What are
you going to do? Not one of those big ones. You can't drive
one of those big ones. You're a banker.'

"The reaction that I've got has just been unbelievable.
But there's so many women out here doing it."

The reaction she gets from A.J. isn't always to her liking.
Since A.J. owns the truck along with his wife, Margaret,
who once rode with her husband but has since decided to
stay at home and tend the house, not to mention a career
as a consultant to trucking companies on matters of safety
compliance and insurance and the like, Helen is techni-
cally a sub-contractor, paid by the mile by A.J. to drive the
truck while he sleeps. But A.J. doesn't always sleep when
Helen drives. And when A.J.'s not sleeping, he is often
clucking at a rough shift or tsk-tsking an unnecessarily
hard application of the brakes or out-and-out criticizing
and lecturing his co-pilot over this flaw or that in her
driving technique.

Their partnership is atypical. Most teams consist of
either two men, father-son platoons or commercial part-
ners, or a married couple. The conjugal co-pilots are
becoming more and more common, which is causing a
seismic shift in trucking culture. Once the sole domain of
scruffy men, it's now not unusual to see trucks parked with
baskets of flowers hanging from the side-view mirrors – a
road-weary woman's nod to homey decorum I note first-
hand about a half-dozen times during my travels.

A.J. and Helen, who is not married or, to the best of my knowledge, romantically affiliated, often find themselves explaining their relationship.

Says A.J.: "I had a friend about twenty years ago."

"You had a friend?" interrupts Helen.

Continues A.J.: "Yeah, imagine that. And I had an apartment back then and my friend left his wife, and one day he just walked in. I was walking out and I said, 'Where are you going?' He said, 'I'm moving in.' . . . This one here" – A.J. motions toward Helen – "lived upstairs and I knew her from the laundromat and stuff, eh? And that's how my buddy met her."

Says Helen: "We all became friends."

"And then he and her became a non-item a few years back," adds A.J., "but we've still kept in touch."

You can lose track of time when you're on the road, even with a ubiquitous digital clock staring back from the dash. We're about twenty-two hours into our journey, wherein we have stopped for the purchase of 937 litres of diesel, which cost $535 at the Flying J outside of London, Ontario, and which prompted A.J. to say: "That'll get us to Wyoming." We have crossed the border without incident – standing in line for thirty minutes to hand paperwork to the humourless U.S. customs officer – and A.J. has explained the bureaucracy; how the slightest error in the reams of required documents can delay a shipment by several hours at a customs officer's whim. We have taken the long way around Detroit and taken secondary roads

around that Chicago gridlock. And we have driven toward
a black sky smattered with zigzag cracks of lightning frequent enough to read by, a stormy prairie night transforming slowly into a calm dawn.

Now, on this Monday morning, we are stopped at a
Flying J Travel Center in Iowa for the team's daily ablu-
tions. A.J. says, "We shower every day." And so I grab my
gear as A.J. leads me through the convenience store, past
the bustling video-game arcade, and down a hallway. He
stops at a machine that looks not unlike an automated
teller. He inserts a card – his Flying J points card – and
retrieves from a slot the slip of paper he hands me. It is, I'm
told, a shower voucher. "Wait until your number is called,"
says A.J. And over the P.A. I hear it: "Shower number 16 is
now ready." I punch in my shower PIN number on the
keypad beside door no. 16. I enter and observe: beige tiles.
Clean floor. Standard-issue blue towel and a bar of soap
wrapped in paper, which I promptly drop in the toilet as I
prepare to bathe.

Before long, clean and sated by a quick breakfast of
eggs and toast, we walk through the parking lot to rejoin
the route. As we do, we see a woman stumble out of a green
Peterbilt, its curtains drawn, her hands occupied zipping
up the fly of her faded blue jeans, her white T-shirt still
hiked halfway up her back, revealing a faded tattoo above
the beltline. We're observing her from a trailer-length but
she is walking quickly away from us, away from the truck
stop, toward the worst spots on the acreage. As she ducks

into a row and escapes our view, A.J. says, rather loudly, "Lot lizard!" and laughs.

"It would be nice if they'd dress up for the occasion," he says. "Whatever happened to a little romance, some high heels, and something nice."

Says Helen: "I guess when you're taking your clothes off as often as she does it doesn't matter what you wear."

Prostitution is prevalent enough in North America's truck stops and rest areas that nearly every truck-stop store sells stickers bearing the words: "No Lot Lizards" or, perhaps to dissuade illiterates, a sticker bearing the image of a cigarette-smoking, short-skirt-wearing, high-heel-sporting, handbag-toting, lipsticked lizard with the red slash through it. The stickers are meant to be a deterrent to one of the top-of-the-list pet peeves of many drivers – the middle-of-the-night solicitation of sex services, which can bring with it a slumber-interrupting bang on the door, not to mention the accompanying possibilities of harm. Prostitutes, after all, have been known to rob unsuspecting truckers of their valuables. They've been known to use their encounters to case trucks that will later be ransacked by associated thieves. And they have also been known to perform sex acts to simply survive another day of a squalid existence.

Jill Leighton, whom I contact in the days after my trip with A.J. and Helen, is a flight attendant these days, and in her spare time she works as a counsellor to prostitutes who'll listen to her words of experience. Kicked out of her home at age fourteen, she was befriended by a man who would soon turn on her. After making like a friend, the man kidnapped and forcibly confined her. A Catholic girl from a small New England town, with an IQ she estimates at 146, she spent more than three years under her captor's control, leaving his watch only to earn him money by turning tricks, often for truckers in California.

"I was an outcall hire, meaning the trucker called from the truck stop, described his truck to my pimp, and I went there to fill his bondage fantasy," she says. "Most prostitutes working truck stops pretty much just work truck stops and do the standard things expected from a prostitute, meaning blow jobs, vaginal sex, etcetera. It is usually women who are runaway teens . . . I've worked as a counsellor with some prostitutes that worked truck stops. And having moved across country a few times, have seen it myself. It's prevalent at virtually every truck stop that doesn't deliberately try to run them off. Pretty much where there are men who are away from their wives and families, there will be prostitutes."

Her mission, she says, is to make it known that prostitutes are human beings, that they're not solely drug-addicted nymphomaniacs who enjoy the gig, that there is often harm being done in the sex trade. She says she's for decriminalization over legalization; the word among prostitutes is that Nevada, which allows legalized prostitution in ten counties with populations under four hundred thousand, also allows decrepit conditions in its state-sanctioned brothels.

"My experience with truckers was like my experience with other tricks in the sense that I was specifically being hired to be submissive to a man with a thing for sadism. I, or better stated, my pimp, was being paid by men who wanted a girl they could hurt, humiliate, and act out their domination-sadistic fantasies with, a girl who played the role of wanting it. Which is probably different than the average prostitute who goes to a trucker, gives him a blow job, or sex and gets X amount of money. I remember many instances of being bound, gagged, and for all intents and purposes raped by truckers fulfilling their sadistic fantasies. Some liked to cover my face with a pillow and climaxed only when I lost consciousness. But this isn't an attempt to say that all truckers are bad. They aren't. I know many kind men who are truckers. Nor is this saying truckers were worse than any other client. They weren't . . . When I initially ran away from home before I was a prostitute, I ran into some kind truckers that gave me a ride, food, and stern lectures that I should not be hitchhiking at my age and at night."

Back on the road in the burgundy Freightliner, we're making an afternoon of watching Iowa's cornfields turn into Nebraska's cornfields, the silvery sway of the stalks in bright sunlight. I tell A.J. about how, on the way to the Monarch headquarters, my rear bumper was nearly mangled by what I thought was an overzealous Peterbilt hauling a pneumatic tanker. I passed the guy within the law, signalled both lane changes, zipped by him at 120 km/h when he appeared to be going far slower. But suddenly when I got

in front of him, he sped up, placing his menacing grill in
my rear-view mirror, giving me more than a little grief.
This alarmed me for a number of reasons, not the least of
which was my knowledge that the tanker this trucker was
hauling could be used to haul almost any kind of dry or
liquid product, from agricultural chemicals to petrochemi-
cals to who knows what. A.J. nods sympathetically.

"You get frustrated, we get frustrated," he says. "As a
trucker, you try and keep a safe zone between you and the
car in front of you. You back off, but then somebody comes
in front of you. You back off more, then the next guy passes
you and fills that space you left. Then people wonder,
'Well, why is that truck on my ass?' Well, it's because there's
been five cars in front of you that've done the same thing.
I say, 'Okay, that's it, there's nobody else coming in. I'm
going to stay on your butt.' And a lot of times that's why
trucks tailgate."

Soon it is raining on the plains and as cars whiz by –
many of them without their lights on despite the grey conditions – A.J. shakes his head.

"People, I always say they're ignorant, but it's not
because they're ignorant-ignorant, it's because they're
ignorant-stupid. There's two ignorants, right?" he says. "It's
not their fault. Same as when people pass us on the right.
They're not doing it on purpose. It's not because they're
ignorant. It's because they're *ignorant*. They just don't
know. It just bugs me."

There are other things that bug him. It bugs him that
officers of the U.S. Department of Transportation carry

guns. "Are we that bad a people, us truck drivers?" he says. It bugs him that Québécois drivers, in his experience, have an affection for outfitting their trucks with flashy paint jobs (metallic purples and turquoises are not uncommon) and eye-catching LED lights. "I don't know what it is with those guys. It's like they're saying, 'I'm here. Look at me.'"

And it bugs him that more people don't listen to one of his favourite radio talk shows, the one hosted by Tom Leykis.

"He has this thing, it's called Flash Friday. You're supposed to drive with your headlights on and girls will come along and flash you. People often talk about it on the CB, 'Hey, turn your lights on, it's Flash Friday.' So on Fridays, if you have your lights on, the girl, if she listens to the same radio show, she'll flash you. It's a pretty lewd show. I've never had a girl actually flash me."

A.J. laughs long and loud, and from behind the curtain I can hear Helen groan. He takes the cue to tone down the discourse, talk a little business.

"It's so cutthroat," says A.J., and now he's speaking about the trucking industry at large. "A guy's mother will die and leave him $300,000 and he can go out and buy five trucks, $20,000 down on each one, and all of a sudden he's in business. All of a sudden, he's a trucking company. He figures, 'Well, Monarch's hauling it for $800. I can do it for $700, I betcha.' He has no idea what his costs are. And a lot of times, companies will give it to him. It makes it bad on the rest of us. Do you match the rate? Monarch won't do that. Somebody comes in, cuts the rate, fine, let 'em have it. A lot of times we'll get the customer back, because they can't give the service we can."

As A.J. spoke I thought about my meeting with one of the proprietors of Monarch Linehaul, a man named Victor Schmidt, with whom I'd met earlier that summer at the company's headquarters just west of Toronto, overlooking Canada's busiest highway. I arrived to find Schmidt standing in the parking lot, wearing a crisp white shirt with a floral tie and grey pants, sucking on a cigarette in the smoggy haze of late June. The highway, a stone's throw away, was four lanes of dull hum, the vehicles quick blurs between the trees.

Schmidt led me into his office, where the floor was tiled in white ceramic, the windows covered in pale venetian blinds. He wore a silver bracelet on his right wrist, a gold-faced Gucci watch on his left. He told me first about his former career as a driver, about how, in the late 1970s and early 1980s, he'd do a run to Florida and then, on a few days' rest, make his way to California. The hustling caught up with him. On November 18, 1982, at about 2:30 a.m., he lost control of his truck near Moose Jaw, Saskatchewan, and rolled the rig to a crumpled stop.

"What scared me about that accident is that I don't remember being really tired," he said. "I don't know whether I was asleep, but it's one of those situations where you're not falling asleep, but you're not thinking properly."

He was thinking, these days, about the possibilities of expanding his company's business to the United States. Monarch was currently moving automotive products for a major Canadian retailer, not to mention luxury items such as vintage automobiles and the high-end kitchen that A.J. and Helen would turn out to be hauling on our journey.

"We once moved twelve trailer loads of those kitchens to Trump Tower in New York City," said Schmidt. "People are paying twenty thousand dollars a kitchen, they don't want the driver walking up in a dirty T-shirt and grease-stained jeans. I don't want our guys in track pants and T-shirts. I want them in a Monarch golf shirt and khaki pants."

The business, indeed, had changed.

"In the seventies, you could take a load to the U.S., come home empty, and still make money," he said. "There's no way you can come home empty and make any money at it any more. You have to concentrate on a laneway and be good at that laneway. For us, that laneway right now more than anything is California.

"They say freight traffic is going to double in the next ten years. When I look at that, I think by this fall we're going to be short of trucks around here."

Carl Cornelius, speaking to me over the phone from his Texas office sometime later, is worried about being short on fuel. In his two-decade entrepreneurial career, Cornelius had done a few things that attract some attention and generate sales and carve out a life. One day in 1979, he walked into a Dallas stockbroker's office in torn dungarees and proposed buying a seventeen-hundred-acre tract of land thirty-five miles south of the city with no downpayment. And once he owned that land, under that unusual condition, he began to build on it, constructing a truck stop after listening to CB dispatches that lamented the absence of a good one in the area. He became frustrated with living under the auspices of a local government that banned the sale of alcohol in its environs. So Cornelius found out what was required to incorporate a new township – 201 people, it turns out, living in the area for six months – and after rustling up a fleet of trailer homes and selling property to family and other folks with no downpayment, it wasn't long before the six months was up and Carl's Corner, Texas, became a place on the map where a man could get a stiff drink with his diesel.

Such was the vision of a dreamer who also once observed the preponderance of pot bellies on the truckers he served and invented Carl's Potbellied Western Shirt, expressly tailored to fit over assorted paunch sizes. Such was the spunky charisma of a well-travelled Texan who'd been both a Christian missionary and a U.S. soldier and who could call Willie Nelson, the country singer, a friend and Albert, prince of Monaco, an acquaintance. The former was a card- and domino-playing pal who, when the truck stop burned down in the late 1990s, held a benefit concert that cued the rebuilding. The latter stopped by once for a look-see, extending an open invitation for a visit to the monied Mediterranean principality. But by 2004, Cornelius had lost his enthusiasm for the truck-stop trade. He'd also lost three sons in the previous six years, two by complications from their lifelong affliction with hemophilia, another to suicide after a diagnosis of schizophrenia. Cornelius was the founder, the mayor, and the judge of Carl's Corner. He was also, at age sixty-four, ready to shut the door on the truck stop where he'd done everything from work the fryers to keep the books to mop the floor. He was ready to play more golf.

But then he got a call from an old friend, Nelson, who asked Cornelius if he'd heard of biodiesel. Cornelius hadn't, but he had faith in Nelson's vision. And so by August 2005, Carl's Corner was back in business, selling BioWillie, a diesel fuel made from soybeans, in an era in which the United States depends heavily on foreign fossil fuels and oil companies are being accused of gouging truckers and motorists alike with record prices at the pump.

"Truckers love it. They're telling me they're getting more miles per gallon. The engine runs cooler. The engine runs quieter. It cleans the engine and the fuel tank and everything out, injectors and all of it. And they say it's got more pulling power. The diesel engine was designed to run off of vegetable oil. So this is just going back to Day One, using what it was designed to run on."

BioWillie is but one variation on a growing theme. Rudolph Diesel, indeed, designed his famous engine in 1897 to run on renewable agricultural resources, specifically peanut oil, a fact that seems to have been largely forgotten for most of the twentieth century, when petroleum-based diesel was the overwhelming choice of diesel consumers. But diesel engines can, indeed, run without modifications on fuels concocted from a wide variety of organic matter, all while reducing greenhouse-gas emissions, not to mention the reliance on foreign oil. Biodiesel usage in the

United States has taken off, growing from 500,000 gallons in 1999 to 25 million gallons in 2004. Estimates pegged 2005 sales at more than double the 2004 number, thanks in large part to tax incentives for users. The fuel has been slower to catch on in Canada, where such tax breaks aren't yet available. Cornelius, for his part, says he has a hard time keeping up with demand.

"I'm about to run out. I'm trying to get some in. There are so many people going to it, we're going to need more biodiesel plants. I haven't been able to do anything with all these calls. Europe is pretty interested in this, too, now. So I've got many, many e-mails. I'm trying to answer them all, but it takes an act of God to get it done."

Cornelius has been less busy, and he's been other things. The son of a kindergarten-teacher mother and deputy-sheriff father who grew up in nearby Hillsboro, Texas, he was a shrimper and a labourer. He was briefly the proprietor of a strip club that he shut down after a reconsideration of its moral implications. He has never been a trucker.

"But I've found out they're some of the most intelligent people in the world," he says. "They've got to be a rolling chartered accountant. They've got to be a rolling mechanic. They've got to be everything to be successful. Marketing, advertising – they've got to do everything to make a living."

He's self-made, to be sure. And much of the making was done in that one day in 1979.

"I saw a newspaper ad, eighteen hundred acres for sale down here. So I went up to Dallas, Texas, and walked into

Mr. Wyatt's office, he worked for Smith Barney. He said, 'What can I do for you?' And I said, 'I want to buy your property in Hill County.' I said, 'How much you want for an acre?' And he told me and I said, 'That's fine.' I said, 'What interest?' And I said, 'That's fine.' And he said, 'Well, let's talk about downpayment.' And I said, 'Nothing down.' He said, 'What?' I said, 'Nothing down. I want immediate possession. I want to close in six months, and I want my first payment a year from the closing.' He said, 'You want to tie up my property for eighteen months?' I said, 'Yeah.' He said, 'You've got to be crazy.' I said, 'I'm sorry to take your time. I thought I presented it to you pretty good.' And I was getting up to walk out and he said, 'Carl, I'll do it.' So I bought it. It's been a success story ever since."

BioWillie is enjoying early success. Nelson uses nothing else on his tour bus. Truckers tend to choose blends of BioWillie and petroleum-based diesel. Carl's Corner sells a blend that's 60 per cent traditional diesel and 40 per cent BioWillie. They also sell an 80-20 blend.

The search for non-traditional means to power the world's trucks and cars and buses is only intensifying. Montana governor Brian Schweitzer has suggested using a process developed in Germany and used by the Nazis during the Second World War that converts coal into clean-burning diesel fuel. The process, which was invented by researchers Franz Fischer and Hans Tropsch, employs gasified coal to produce paraffin wax that is suitable for refining into a synthetic oil that can in turn be refined into diesel or propane or butane, to name a few of the possibilities. Germany, which sits on scarce oil but boasts coal in quantity, used the technique to make diesel and airplane fuel in the wake of the Allied forces' successful blockade of petroleum throughout the war. Ditto South Africa, which survived the turn of the world's cold shoulder during its apartheid era by using the process that still, with production at approximately two hundred thousand barrels a day, supplies about a quarter of the nation's fuel requirements.

China, which produces and consumes more coal than any other country, has invested billions in the technology. Sasol, a company that set up shop in South Africa, has recently partnered with the country of Qatar in building a plant that will, by converting natural gas to diesel in a method also invented by Fischer and Tropsch, produce what is being billed as the world's cleanest diesel.

There are other alternatives. A couple of Ontario trucking companies agreed to purchase ten trucks that burn natural gas from Vancouver's Cummins Westport, Inc. The engines boast 50 per cent lower emissions of particulate matter and greenhouse gases.

But biofuels are perhaps more attractive in the long term because they rely on renewable resources instead of fossil fuels. Soybeans aren't the only raw material that can be used in concocting diesel. There is a plant in Missouri that uses the waste from a nearby turkey-processing plant – everything from the feathers to the bones – to make the fuel it sells to a nearby factory that uses it to generate power. Kits are available to convert the Volkswagen diesel in your driveway into a Beetle that runs on the used cooking oil from your neighbourhood pub's fryer. Diner proprietors who once had to pay a disposal service to truck away their old oil are, if they're enterprising, able to find willing buyers for the gunk. Malaysia, the world's biggest producer of crude palm oil, is building two biodiesel plants to make fuel from the exotic trees that adorn its landscape. Environmentalists point out that many of the countries that signed on to the Kyoto Protocol in a race to reduce greenhouse-gas emissions by 2012 are increasing their commitment to palm-based diesel. The European Union, for instance, has mandated that its diesel must contain 5.75 per cent of biodegradable oil by 2010, up from 2.5 per cent.

The catch is that many of the biofuels only become cost effective – even with oil prices on the rise – when government tax incentives are attached to its usage, as they are in the United States and Europe.

Overzealous drivers in Europe, where biodiesel is more popular and where more people own diesel-powered automobiles, have been said to pour vegetable oil straight into their tanks, which isn't recommended. The car will run, but not for long. Vegetable oil that hasn't been refined for engines can damage fuel pumps and various internal components. As of 2005, biofuels supplied an estimated 1 per cent of the world's energy demands. Still, proponents point to a groundswell of enthusiasm for modes of power generation that don't involve invading Middle Eastern countries or opening up Alaskan wildlife preserves to exploration.

As Schweitzer has said: "We can do it cheaper than importing oil from the sheiks, dictators, rats, and crooks that we're bringing it in from right now." Cornelius sees it the same way, but he expects friction from the folks in the oil business.

"Of course they're going to fight this. They don't want you to get into their honey hole," he says. "Would you want someone to get in your honey hole if you were making $9.5 billion in profits, or whatever it is? You're up against it all the time. Hell, you think they can't build an automobile that'll last a lifetime? My uncle used to be an executive vice president at General Motors years ago. He'd say to me, 'You think we can't build something that'll last a lifetime?' You don't make your money selling the cars. You make it on the parts. The cars are designed to break down. But it can't continue like this."

Cornelius, for his part, can't continue this interview. Not long ago on the precipice of retirement, he's now busier than he's ever been. He's working on a deal to build a biodiesel plant that will power his truck stop and keep the pumps flowing. He just met with a group of businessmen who say they want to put the Carl's Corner name on truck stops around the United States. On top of that, he's got fires to put out at home.

"My wife's madder than a wet hen right now," Cornelius says, chuckling. "The cook didn't show up so she had to cook in the restaurant. She wanted the day off. But all of us fill in where we're needed . . . I'm tired. I go to sleep at midnight and get up at three in the morning. I could take a nap right now. But my naps don't last fifteen minutes. I'm beating myself in the butt, you know what I mean. I've got to get a couple of good people to help me. But you asked how I feel? I feel like a pig in mud. That's total happiness."

A.J.'s five-hour shift is up, and he's climbing into the bunk, not at all self-conscious in white briefs and white socks. Helen, meanwhile, is rejoining the highway with the ease of an old-timer, completely ignoring the presence of the half-naked man who's zipping the curtain and heading for bed.

"I didn't want to fail at this," she says. "For a long time, I didn't want to tell anyone I was becoming a truck driver. A.J. knew, and his wife, and that was basically it. And then my sister came from Kapuskasing for a visit . . . When I told her, she was in shock. Total shock. 'Are you crazy? Do you know how hard it is to drive one of those trucks? Why would you give up your job at the bank?' My other sister, she still says to me, 'If you can do it, I can still get out of this rat race and I can do it.' She still calls me up and her first words to me are, 'I'm so proud of you. I'm so proud of you.'

"My oldest daughter, the one in Whitehorse, she's a little gypsy. She was so excited about me doing this. She's a waitress and she said, 'Every time someone came in the restaurant today I had to tell them about my mother.'"

We're rolling through Wyoming now. The landscape, once flat, has contours. In a valley there's a line of railway cars streaming east. And as we move west, we pass signs for place names familiar and not: Laramie, Elk Mountain, Rawlins, Riner, Red Desert, Table Rock, Rock Springs, Green River, Evanston. A.J. has passed these signs hundreds of times, but he knows these destinations as map dots. At one time, before the interstate highways were laid out, the truckers knew the main streets. The cross-country route that preceded I-80, the Lincoln Highway, didn't bypass cities and towns as much as it connected them. But as Larry McMurtry, the Pulitzer Prize–winning author of *Lonesome Dove*, points out in his fine book *Roads*, the interstate isn't the spiritual descendant of the great two-lane routes such as the Lincoln and Highway 66. The interstate has its roots in another mode of transport.

"The great roads of nineteenth-century America were the rivers of the Americas: the Hudson, the St. Lawrence, the Delaware, the Susquehanna, the Monongahela, the Ohio, the Arkansas, the Columbia, the Red River of the North, the Rio Grande, and of course, the Missouri-Mississippi. . . . For a road, like a river, very often merely passes through long stretches of countryside, having little effect on the lives of people who live only a few miles from it. When I lay abed as a boy in our ranch house, listening to those trucks growl their way up highway 281, the sound of those motors came to seem as organic as the sounds of the various birds and animals who were apt to make noises in the night. . . . The sounds of the road were part of the complex symphony of country life. Yet we had little to do with that road. . . . The roads are just there, routes to migrate along, if it's time to migrate."

As we drift west on the high-banked river, we pass a preponderance of cattle trucks driving east. A.J. points out that much of the beef that will end up on plates along the

Atlantic coast travels this road. He says cattle trucks don't mind starting their journeys a little overweight, as the journey's natural course will send untold pounds of dung off the side of the trailer and onto the road. He says it's a little known fact that all along Interstate 80, you can actually trace the trail of the eastbound cattle haulers headed for Chicago's slaughterhouses. They leave behind a line of manure flattened by tires. It is thicker in some places than others, caked to the road like discarded bubblegum.

We take a turn off I-80 in the heat of the early afternoon, along a ramp and down a parallel service road to the parking lot of a middle-of-nowhere tourist attraction. It's a museum dedicated to the great migration to the American West. "Professional tourists, that's what some people call us," says Helen. We walk in, pay the admission, take the escalator past the animatronic Indians and animals, and tour the exhibits.

Deciding time is not an issue, Helen also requests a stop at Cabela's, a big-box outfitter a few hours down the road in Kearney, Nebraska, that serves America's fishing-rod-and-gun fetish. It's thirty-five-thousand square feet of hunting rifles, crossbows, rods and reels, ammunition, motorized duck-hunting decoys, and, as the centrepiece, a savannah's worth of trophy kills of antelopes and big cats and other creatures that once roamed the wilds of Africa and Canada and elsewhere. It's a taxidermist's masterwork, but A.J. and Helen, who have been here before, take little notice of the scene and carry on about their business. We agree to meet at the exit in half an hour; the place is big

enough that I won't run into A.J. until the appointed time.
Helen, on the other hand, crosses my path a few minutes
later. She is looking for a gift for a grandchild and, passing
over the outstanding selection of toy firearms and sling-
shots, selects a small plastic fishing rod.

And I am off to peruse more exotic offerings. They sell
no-bark collars for hunting dogs, a device designed to
deliver an electric shock when activated by the vibrations
of canine vocal cords, "so your dog punishes himself when
he barks," says the literature. They sell do-it-yourself taxi-
dermy packages (the deer-jaw extractor is $14.99 while
the squirrel-mounting kit – "an interesting touch to any
sportsman's room" – is $17.99). They sell instant stick
camouflage face tape. They sell the M.A.D. Wildlife Eye
Video System, a heat-and-motion-detecting surveillance
rig that allows hunters to get to know the habits of the
local deer without the hassle of actually sitting and waiting
outdoors. A testimonial from a famous big-buck hunter
called it "the single most significant improvement in
hunting equipment, EVER!" Surely he was forgetting about
guns, which are on offer in quantity, from squirrel rifles to
circa-1874 old-west replicas to state-of-the-art, miss-and-
you're-a-moron super-shooters complete with red-dot laser
sights and optical scopes and military-calibre ammunition.

As we approach the California border, A.J. insists that
we treat ourselves to the Flying J's famous buffet, which he
also insists on referring to as the "barffet," as in "It'll make
you barf, eh?" He has more than enough Flying J points to
pay for three meals.

Flying J is the corporate ruler of the truck-wise fuel-and-food business, but there might not be a truck stop on this continent that compares to the Autohof Strohofer, an oasis of rare luxury on the outskirts of Munich, Germany. It's the biggest in Europe. It has the requisite twenty-four-hour restaurant, a butcher shop selling, along with the meat, gift baskets and snacks. It has a Burger King with Internet access. It has a fully licensed mechanic for cars and trucks. It has a truck wash, a steam room, a sauna, a swimming pool, a casino, a multi-faith temple, a so-called life park that amounts to a grassy area for taking a walk.

European sophistication knows no limits. Italian truck stops serve freshly pressed panini oozing with mortadella and mozzarella. In France one can buy the fruits of Beaujolais' finest village appellations. At Brasserie Gares des Routiers, a truckers' haven in Floriac, the steak filets are served seared on the outside and rare within, garnished with peach and gravy. The cheese – Camembert, ripe – is served as a main-course follow-up. The wine goes without saying. In a country that savours its meals, even the roadside restaurants rise to the occasion. There is little so exotic on this side of the Atlantic, although Starbucks, the Seattle coffee-shop company that made its name by up-selling urbanites from their usual one-dollar coffees to four-dollar cappuccinos and the like, has begun an expansion in rural America, hoisting a fifty-foot-tall sign amongst those of Waffle House and McDonald's and the Flying J, just off an exit of Interstate 20 in Alabama. There are those who don't see the wisdom in the move: "Small-town America is clearly Dunkin' Donuts land, and I think Starbucks coffee is too strong for rural America," one industry analyst told the Boston *Globe*.

The buffet is truly an expansive spread, available at each and every one of the Flying J's ubiquitous outlets, four of which are in Canada, at all hours, on every day of the year. Almost unfailingly, the choices include roast beef, fried chicken, French fries, mashed potatoes, pork chops, beef gravy, something called white sausage gravy, a medley of vegetables, and a dessert table that includes chocolate cake, some sort of red-berry pie, various cookies, and a soft-serve machine that provides the icy base for the massive fudge-covered sundaes with which many of the attending truckers cap their meals. There's a salad bar, too. It takes me a while to decide how to fill my plate. A large man in overalls, to whom, I realize, I am a roadblock on the way to more beef, senses my indecision and says, "It'll still be here if you come back."

Obesity has been called an epidemic among North Americans, and some truckers are among North America's behemoths. Their sedentary lifestyle, combined with the traditional fare of their habitual haunts, makes them a generally portly bunch. There are entrepreneurs who figure there's money to be made in installing fitness equipment in truck stops. At least one Canadian stop is outfitted with coin-operated treadmills. But as I return to the table, my plate heaping, I wonder how many penny-pinching truckers – who have it in their genes to believe getting more food for less money is a daily coup – are willing to pay a dollar for the chore of power-walking in place for a half-hour.

I sit down, nearly spilling my load. Helen is looking perturbed, A.J. bemused. I catch the tail end of a sentence. She says something about marriage.

"I never asked you to marry me," says A.J., shaking his head. "Well, maybe in your dreams."

"Yeah," says Helen, "marriage wasn't exactly what you had in mind."

I don't know what to make of their relationship: a single woman and a married man sharing week after week on a lonely road, the man often stripping to his underwear without a hint of self-consciousness, the woman weathering a steady stream of horny chatter.

"If I was a woman and I found my husband with another man, that'd be it," A.J. says, and by now we're digesting the buffet forty miles up the road. "But if I'm a man, which I am, and I come home and find my wife in bed with another woman, I'd want to join in. It'd be perfectly okay. Why is it one way for one thing and another way for another?"

Helen rolls her eyes. After another long night, San Francisco, hidden under its morning blanket of fog, is on the horizon. A.J. pulls the truck into the docklands, finds the warehouse that's expecting the kitchen shipment, and I help the truckers unload their cargo. The journey's end is, for me, an airport not far away. We drive through another California traffic jam, past farms of shushing wind turbines.

Squinting into the sun, marvelling at a landscape that's as
familiar as it is distant, A.J. extends a hand to the horizon
and says, "Welcome to paradise."

Three summers later, A.J. is standing amid the dust and
the hum of a factory that makes kitchen cabinets.

"I'm in the big leagues now," he says. "I'm out on my
own."

It's been eight months since A.J. left Monarch and took
a job as the principal truck driver for a local manufac-
turer of high-end cabinetry. He says he's making nearly
twice as much as he was making for Monarch, "finally
making what I think I'm worth." He has done what the
minority of prosperous truckers all do – found a niche,
performed impeccably, managed his costs, and held out
for an employer that would pay a premium for his profes-
sionalism. He's making a lot more money than the average
hauler because he shows up to the doorsteps of luxury
showrooms wearing a clean pressed shirt and a smile. And
the benefits run deeper than his bank account. He also
knows his schedule as many as a few months in advance.
He's home on weekends. He's ecstatic – and his wife is
getting accustomed.

Says Margaret, who is seeing her husband with more
regularity than she ever has in their eighteen-year marriage: "It's a change. It's an adjustment. Because you're so
used to being independent and doing everything yourself.
Now he's back and . . . we actually can almost have a life

now. You can enjoy your home and try to have friends and entertain and be more in touch with people.

"It's pretty nice. He can be a human being now, instead of being a robot."

She knew what she was getting into. They met when Margaret was a dispatcher for another local company and A.J. was the resident friend-to-all glad-hander. He was beloved around the company in part for his sense of humour. Once, when he was hauling heavy construction equipment on a flatbed trailer, he was returning from a delivery with an empty trailer. So he bought a Tonka-sized excavator, the kind a two-year-old would play with, and strapped it to the middle of the vast flatbed. It caused traffic chaos, cars with kids whizzing by, only to slam on the brakes to do a double-take.

They both say they hated each other at first. "He was a candy-ass. Everybody loved him," says Margaret.

Says A.J.: "I had everybody fooled. She's the one who really knows me."

They connected and married. And just as quickly, A.J. was back on the road.

"It wasn't good for us," says Margaret. "It's hard. It takes a very unique person to handle it. She can't be a person who's calling dispatch every day, 'Where's my husband? My dishwasher's broken.' It sounds funny, but it's serious. I remember when I worked in dispatch, people would call up and I'd think, how can a woman be like that? Can't she make up her own mind? But now I see it, it's not good. You become so independent."

A.J. laughs: "I'd come home and I'd want to take the reins, and she'd want to keep driving the buggy herself, eh?"

Margaret is not laughing: "You don't have a choice. He'd come home, he'd be home four hours, and he'd be back out the door to California. It was like, 'Hi. Bye.' I'd pack him a cooler. He'd have a shower. If you're lucky, he'd plow the driveway if it was wintertime. It is an adjustment now, but it's actually a fairly nice adjustment. He deserves to be home. He's worked very hard."

Says A.J.: "I've always said you have to love this job. And I used to. I don't know if I love it still, but there was a time when I wouldn't want to be out of the truck for an hour because I loved it. I missed it. I loved it so much when I first started driving. I like it now."

Their relationship, A.J. tells me in a phone conversation on another day, had rough patches. There was tension brought about by A.J.'s driving with Helen. There was a week where Margaret moved out, bought twenty thousand dollars' worth of furniture and appliances and set up her life in an apartment, only to have A.J. move the stuff back to their house.

"So many things have changed. The industry has changed," says A.J. "When I started, we didn't have logbooks up here in Canada. You just drove and if you got tired, you went to sleep. If you fell asleep – well, you'd probably get charged with careless, but you could just say a deer ran out into the road. When I was a kid, my jaw would drop when a truck drove by. Now I don't love it, but I like it, as long as there's more good days than bad days. And there's lots of good days still. There was a time back in 2001 when I was just about done.

"We were lined up at the Queenston-Lewiston Bridge, and the locals felt so sorry for us that they would pull us into this big field and they had chicken and hot dogs and hamburgers and pop and it was almost like a party atmosphere. There was nothing you could do. They'd take every truck, open it up."

Margaret: "Phones, 24-7, every day of the year. I've even had Christmas calls. I just got a call, one of my drivers hit a bridge. So I'm dealing with them with the insurance company."

Margaret is an independent contractor in the safety-compliance business. She works for a long list of trucking companies, aiding them in hiring and training drivers, coaching them through audits of their driver logs, liaising with insurance companies in the wake of accidents. She recently did work for a company that employed a driver who was arrested for transporting a shipment of marijuana. The driver swore she was innocent, that she'd been set up, and knew nothing of the drugs. But police on the scene made a simple discovery: her cellphone had been used to call the cellphone of the man who'd been caught unloading the weed from her trailer. Margaret had believed the driver, but it wasn't exactly the first time she'd been snowed.

"My theory is I believe everybody. But once you lie to me, it'll be the last time," she says. "I don't want to make the industry look bad because there's good and bad. But thank goodness, overall, the good overcompensates for the bad."

The good, for A.J. these days, is riding solo.

"It's like living in your bathroom when you run team with somebody," he says. "There's husbands and wives that do it for years and years and they love it. I know another couple tried it for a year . . . and they just fought like cats and dogs. They just couldn't make it work. They just fought and fought and fought. She's headstrong, eh? She knew everything right out of school. That was the problem."

His job has a downside. He's the guy who has to unload the cabinets. They're solid wood, mostly, a few hundred pounds frequently, no joy to lug, especially in summer's heat. At a recent delivery he soaked through two shirts and was sweating through a third before he had concluded his heavy labour.

"Most of my friends wouldn't even consider taking this job and they told me I was an idiot for taking it," he says. "It's very driver-unfriendly freight. The first few months, I thought I couldn't do this job. I thought I'd bitten off more than I could chew. I was so sore, I could hardly move. I mean, you get a pantry on there, two of these young fellows can lift it up, but most of the time I've got to take it down by myself. Gravity helps. It's like a controlled crash. I've lost thirteen pounds since I started."

Still, the job makes sense for him, sore muscles and all, because he knows the alternative could be far worse. To find a company that will pay a fair rate – a rate on which a driver can play within most of the rules and still make a profit – is a job in itself, and it only happened for A.J., one could argue, because he spent a career building contacts and cementing his reputation.

"Next week a load broker could come in and say, 'Oh, A.J.'s hauling that load for you for $1,000. I can do it for $600.' The company says, '$600? You've got it.' So the load broker gets on his phone in his little office and he finds somebody stupid or desperate enough to take that load for $600. And he'll start off at $300. So he'll find someone who's maybe going in the right direction, and maybe it's not a full load, so he'll offer it at $300. And he'll put it on the Internet, and he'll get someone who'll call and say, 'I'll take that for $300.' So he's just made $300. So Tuesday comes along, it still hasn't moved, it might move to $350. Wednesday, $375. Thursday, he's getting a little panicky because it's got to move by Friday, so now he's going to pay $450. Come Friday, if he hasn't moved it, he's in big trouble. So he might have to let it go for more than he's getting paid. But as a customer, you don't know who's going to be backing into your dock. The broker just finds someone stupid enough or desperate enough to take the load. It could be unsafe equipment.

"They're a necessary evil, because they're putting freight on your trailer. But they just undercut and undercut. I was in Baltimore and one of these guys wanted someone to take a load. It's 457 miles from here to Baltimore and they wanted to pay $350. That's less than a dollar a mile. You tell 'em to stick it where the sun don't shine for that kind of money. But someone will do it."

Someone will do it, perhaps, because the job can sound
exotic to an outsider. But Tim Anderson, a long-time
trucker, believes there's no truth in advertising in the business of recruiting truck drivers.

"People are led to believe that their first year on the job
they're going to make good money and they're going to see
all these beautiful places and they're going to eat out all the
time. Doesn't that just sound glamorous?" says Anderson.
"Then it turns out they get out there. And they aren't paid
for anything but the mile. So if the truck's not moving,
they're not getting paid. So then they have to compensate
for all the uncompensated time, when they're stuck sitting
around waiting to get loaded, waiting to get unloaded, stuck
in traffic, waiting for the highway to open – all these things
that take away from their earnings. Then they have to work
twice as hard. They're eating truck-stop food. And they're
seeing the Rocky Mountains at three in the morning. If
there was complete disclosure to what these people are
getting themselves into, then yeah, blame the drivers.

"By the time a person makes a career change, they get
out there, they get a licence, they're already in a position of
being financially held hostage. One of the largest carriers in
the country has finally burned through so many groups of
people to bring into their labour pool that they've started
recruiting gay and lesbian teams. And we had to ask, is that
a good thing or is that a bad thing? This is a carrier that
has some iffy anecdotal stories regarding its treatment of
its drivers. I know one driver who worked for them who
ruptured a hernia and he literally had to drive himself to

the hospital in a semi truck because the company wouldn't dispatch an ambulance. His guts are hanging out and he's driving a semi truck down the freeway . . ."

Anderson, the president of the Gay Truckers Association, a U.S. non-profit organization that represents its members and attempts to improve conditions for gay and lesbian truckers, is speaking over the phone from his Pacific Northwest home. A seventeen-year veteran of the gear-jamming business, Anderson hasn't been on the road since a 2002 traffic accident in which his head smashed against a windshield; the accident left him struggling to recover his vision. But the road has given him a rare education in trucking's little-known corners. He's an American but he once drove for a Canadian company that, unbeknownst to him, was smuggling undeclared alcohol in the produce shipments he was hauling. He quit that job when the folks at Canada Customs paid him a call. He has also witnessed other not-so-well concealed transgressions.

"Drivers talk about the five-hundred-mile rule: Once you get five hundred miles from the house, anything goes," says Anderson. "I just had a driver that called me up a couple of weeks ago who was telling me he was fuelling and the guy next to him had these girls he'd pick up and transport around the country, and yet he was married. He said he did this all the time and he was trying to get rid of this girl because he was tired of her and wanted to get somebody else."

Anderson says truck chasers, men and women who seek out truckers with whom to fulfill various sexual fantasies,

have become more common since the popularization of
the Internet.

"It's very common," he says. "A survey was done out
of Arizona State University. They were asking a random
sample of drivers if they were familiar with gay trucker
cruising behaviour. And it was a question they posed that
had the most consistent response . . . Every driver was able
to identify the behaviour although each of them indicated
that they weren't involved in it themselves. Drivers are
lonely and if there was a way that people could meet and
have friendship and share a cup of coffee, that's wonder-
ful. But a lot of times these folks have no interest in
knowing anything about you. They just want to have sex
in a truck."

There are issues over which his group might have some
modicum of control that Anderson is working to rectify.
One of them is a long-time quandary: it has always been
difficult for truck drivers to undergo HIV testing. For one,
you can't park a truck within a reasonable radius of most
hospitals and clinics. For another, most testing facilities
require the subject to return to the site where the test
was administered in two weeks to get the results. Again,
it's a difficult-to-schedule feat for the average trucker and
Anderson, noting the slow pace of progress, chuckles in
frustration.

Trucking and the spread of HIV, after all, have been
linked in a bevy of Third World countries, where it's
common for truckers to behave promiscuously on the
road, often without the protection of a condom, and return

home to share a bed with a spouse. When a professor at the Emory University of Medicine in Atlanta procured a government grant for research on the sexual habits of American truckers, the study was among those challenged by a group of conservative political activists who questioned the value of getting a handle on the sex lives of truckers. No matter that scientists have for years made the connection between truck drivers and the speedy transmission of HIV in sub-Saharan Africa, among other places.

Says Anderson: "Here we are, twenty-five years into this disease. We have studies from all over the world that trucking is one of the primary routes of transmission, especially in developing nations. We know the epidemic gained an incredible foothold in India and in Africa and elsewhere through trucking. These drivers are going to high-risk populations and then they come home to low-risk populations. And there's a percentage of people who are not out. They're heterosexual at home and they're either gay or bisexual when they're on the road. They may be engaging in behaviour that puts their loved ones at risk. And yet no one has ever talked about this in the trucking community in North America. And yet we've got 3 million truckers in the States. Even if 5 per cent of them are in this situation, that's a big number."

The study is continuing, but Helen counts herself among those who won't be particularly interested in the results. When her two-year run with A.J. ended, so did her trucking career. She works full-time at a retail store now, counting cash in regular shifts. She's reluctant to talk about the circumstances of her exit from the business with which she once seemed so enamoured.

"I should have got out the first month," she says. "I don't want to discuss what happened or why it happened. I'm just glad to be out of the truck."

One of Helen's biggest issues with the job had nothing to do with her co-driver. She says that as the months wore on she had an increasingly difficult time getting quality sleep in the bunk. Sleeping on the move proved too bumpy. Sleeping while parked in truck stops wasn't so bad, until, say, a refrigerated van parked nearby and she was disturbed by its buzz. Sleeping with ear plugs helped a little.

Despite her restlessness, she somehow managed to keep her eyelids apart when she took the wheel.

"A.J. was always in awe that I was able to finish my shift, that I was still able to drive even though I wasn't sleeping," she says. "I never fell asleep at the wheel. Never. If I was really tired, I'd pull over and get out and walk around for a few minutes and that would pull me through."

But her insomnia got so bad that she says her doctor urged her to quit the job, an order with which she finally complied.

"It was really affecting my health," she says. "I just couldn't keep going the way I was going."

Still, she acknowledges there was something more to her retirement from the road. She's deliberate with her words when she's asked about A.J.

"If I saw him on the street," she says, slowly, "I'd have to walk on the other side."

She retracts that statement a moment later.

"No, maybe not. It's in the past," she says. "There's something good that came out of it. I got to meet people on the road. I got to see the countryside. Some of the teams we drove with, I've kept in touch. I didn't go on the CB and talk to drivers very much, but I listened. I learned a lot about the States. I learned a lot about the different mountains. I can go on *Jeopardy!* and get some of the questions that I wouldn't have ever known."

Afterword

I heard my favourite trucking song in the middle of a distant city where trucks don't exist as we know them. In London, the small ones are lorries and the big ones are arties, for articulated vehicles, or juggernauts. In the British Isles, a cross-country hauler, at least to the eye of a toiler of the North American road, is a local pickup and delivery guy. And maybe that's why the Brits have always counted among themselves aficionados of Americana. Just as the new world has its anglophiles, so does the old have its worshippers of the new.

Or at least that was my experience on the night years ago when I saw a name in the music listings with which I was vaguely familiar. I'd heard of Townes Van Zandt, the country singer-songwriter, not because I had some great appreciation for the purity of the kind of old-time music they don't make in Nashville any more or because I knew a lot of his songs. He'd shared some bills with a Toronto band, the Cowboy Junkies, and I knew he'd written a song, "Pancho and Lefty," of which Willie Nelson once did a cover. And so I wandered down to the club around tea time and attempted to buy a ticket to the show. Word from the ticket booth was that the proprietors couldn't, in good conscience, sell me a ticket to the show. They couldn't, in good conscience, sell anyone a ticket to the show, mostly because they hadn't heard from Townes Van Zandt in quite some time, and they weren't sure whether he was even coming to put on a show. Try back later, was the advice handed down from the window. And so I did.

Well, it turns out Mr. Van Zandt made it to the club. But there seemed to be some doubt about whether he would actually make it to the stage. He could barely walk as he emerged from the backstage black into the spotlight, limping and plunking down on the chair he would occupy the rest of the night. He couldn't really sing – that is, if you're of the mind that singers should be able to stay in key and in time – his voice a tuneless rasp that wavered and slurred and hiccupped. He couldn't play guitar – his picking hand trembled visibly as he botched notes and his fretting hand was crudely patched with dangling medical tape and Popsicle sticks, which he would explain later as the remedy for at least one injured digit.

You'd think a performer, sitting in front of a couple of hundred people with those handicaps – no legs, no voice, and sub-punk guitar skills – might struggle to make the evening memorable for anything but the flurry of boos that drove him from the stage. You'd think this man would surely bomb. But Van Zandt charmed. He charmed in the stories he spun. He charmed in the self-deprecating jokes he told (he said he had three kids, aged twenty-seven, fourteen, and five. "I don't get laid much," he cracked, "but when I do, it works"). And he charmed in the songs he sang, or bellowed, really. Maybe you couldn't make out the melodies. Maybe he couldn't embellish the spare odes with fancy picking in the way he once had. But he had his words, and he had his gut. And he delivered a performance that left the audience, judging by their hushed fixation and their loud ovations, enthralled.

Near show's end – not before he had pointed out a handful of times that he had to get off the stage because the club was transforming into a disco to service the late-night party crowd – he introduced a song that is about, to the best of anyone's analysis, either big trucks or the life-swallowing demons of the on-the-move musician. "White Freightliner Blues" isn't as clever as a lot of trucking songs in the canon. It isn't as tuneful as "Roll Truck Roll," Red Simpson's take on the loneliness of a bad-weather Western swing. It isn't as catchy as, say, "Convoy," C.W. McCall's tale of highway-patrol defiance that sold over 10 million copies and inspired a film starring Kris Kristofferson and Ali McGraw. It was never a hit like "Six Days on the Road," Dave Dudley's ode to the endless black ribbon, which hit No. 2 on the country charts in 1963, or "Drivin' My Life Away" by Eddie Rabbit, which was in heavy mainstream radio rotation in the 1980s. And it's not a Canadian treasure like "Bud the Spud," the Stompin' Tom Connors paean to a potato hauler from Prince Edward Island. In Stompin' Tom's world, the bears are perpetually looking for the notorious truck that is rearranging the asphalt on Highway 401. But Bud's shining bolt can never be had.

"White Freightliner Blues" is a blues, which, considering the subject matter gives it a leg up on any song that's not a blues. It has a simple central image: The narrator states an intention to inhabit the side of a highway, simply to be in the presence of the big rigs, to hear their grunts and moans and burps. The song has been interpreted in some quarters as an ode to heroin, or the white illegal substance of Van Zandt's choice when he wrote the tune. And surely Van Zandt wasn't being literal in his assertion. Surely he wasn't an enthusiast of standing on the shoulder and staring at motorized giants. As David Byrne, the singer for the defunct rock band Talking Heads, wrote in his online journal in 2005, "gazing at traffic going by an ordinary stretch is seen as the pastime of a psychopath." But as Byrne elaborated in an entry, it's curious that rivers are seen as aesthetically beautiful while highways are not.

"Why shouldn't a highway be perceived more or less the same way [as a river]?" Byrne wrote. "The never-ending flow of cars . . . has a similar constant variation, more or less like a river, and it remains more or less one thing, like a river . . . So aren't they more or less the same?"

Byrne wondered if there was some built-in prejudice in humans to view the man-made creations as impure next to nature's splendour. Indeed, some of us do. And perhaps it's because, in so many places, the highway is built without heed to aesthetics. As Larry McMurtry points out in *Roads*, the U.S. interstate system's goal "is to move you, not educate you." McMurtry, marvelling at the highways that weave together his vast nation, pinpoints their efficiency. "What made it possible to travel that distance . . . was the great road itself, a highway designed for just that type of travel. I never had to go more than one hundred yards off the highway for food, gasoline, and a rest room." McMurtry, of course, is hardly a romantic of William Least Heat-Moon proportions. The latter is the writer of *Blue Highways*, a travelogue of the secondary thoroughfares that are often marked in blue on American maps, the roads big trucks mostly leave alone these days. The former calls truckers "the last free men alive, the true cowboys of the road."

In any event, "White Freightliner Blues" wasn't the only tune Van Zandt wrote that could pass for a trucking song. The first line of "Pancho and Lefty," perhaps his best-known song, possesses an ingrained weariness that every follower of the white line can appreciate. And there are others, including "Highway Kind," that speak to a lust for the lonely road, the journey-as-destination pursuit. Count Van Zandt among the many songwriters who've found beauty and ugliness and metaphor among the diesel stacks. Every form of institutionalized transportation has its appreciation society. The railyards have their trainspotters. The airport landing strips have their binocular-toting voyeurs, just as the seaways have their watchers of ships. Truck drivers have their songwriters. That's not to say truckers actually listen to trucking music any more; it has its audience, but it's a niche market. My cousin was perhaps the exception, but he was hardly the only driver to dabble in the tuneful arts. Dwight Yoakam, the country singer, spent time driving trucks before his career as a musician and an actor took off. One of his most popular songs, which appears to take some inspiration from his continent-crossing experience, was titled "Thousand Miles From Nowhere." Such is the life.

My cousin Lo quit his job as a trucker those years back, but the job never really left him. Not long after, he took a position as a travelling salesman. The surroundings were different, to be sure. He got a company car instead of a rig. He was frustrated with airport hassles more than traffic jams. He slept in high-end hotels instead of a bunk. He ate expense-account steaks and drank expense-account martinis. And he bought his first house, its biggest selling point, the way he put it to me, being the basement fit for a music studio. He got a new band together, started working on new songs. But one thing didn't change. He still wrote a lot of trucking songs. He didn't write travelling-salesman songs.

Acknowledgements

I owe a debt to my cousin Lo, who inspired these journeys, and to the drivers who tolerated my presence and questions. I've been lucky to cross paths with mentors, colleagues, and editors who are as gifted as they are generous, among them Dave Bidini, who suggested I write this book, Roy MacGregor, Chris Young, Chris Jones, Graham Parley, and Ken Whyte. Dinah Forbes and Elizabeth Kribs at McClelland & Stewart were ridiculously patient and supportive, which means a lot and won't be forgotten. Thanks also to Jenny Bradshaw for her eye; to Scott Maniquet for his help in the library; and to Gordon Lightfoot for the title. Most of all I'd like to thank my family: Dad, Scott, Sue, Jen, Brent, James, Will, Terry, Mark, Darcy, and Phil. And Oscar and Andrea, for loving me at home and on the road.

Dave Feschuk, a columnist with the *Toronto Star*, has been a sportswriter since 1994. He has been nominated for a National Newspaper Award, and his piece on the underdog's life of Wayne Gretzky's hockey-playing brothers was cited in *The Best American Sports Writing*. This is his first book. He lives with his wife and son in Toronto.